Soul Tattoos
Indelible Milestones and Mortals

Fran Walsh Ward

Halo Publishing International

Soul Tattoos
Indelible Milestones and Mortals
Copyright © 2021 Fran Walsh Ward
All rights reserved.

This book is a memoir. It reflects the author's present recollections of people and experiences over time.

No part of this book may be reproduced in any manner whatsoever without the prior written permission of the publisher, except in the case of brief quotations embodied in reviews.

The views and opinions expressed in this book are those of the author and do not necessarily reflect the official policy or position of Halo Publishing International. Any content provided by our authors are of their opinion and are not intended to malign any religion, ethnic group, club, organization, company, individual or anyone or anything.

ISBN: 978-1-61244-942-5
LCCN: 2020922508

Halo Publishing International, LLC
8000 W Interstate 10, Suite 600
San Antonio, Texas 78230
www.halopublishing.com

Printed and bound in the United States of America

Dedication

For the luminaries in my life.
By shining their light, they
have helped to light my way.

Contents

Dedication	3
Preface	9
Introduction	11
Home	13
Ma	16
Dad	20
Anufra (Uncle Frank)	25
School Days	31
Sister Patricia	33
Mr. Delaney	39
Mr. Burns	44
The Prom	49
The Arts And Sciences	58
Harvard And MIT	60
The Isabella Stewart Gardner Museum	68
Sweet Sixteen	75
Higher Education	81
Dartmouth College	83

My New World — 89
- The Log Cabin — 91
- The White House — 98
- The Foxcroft Student — 106
- The Golf Team — 111
- The College of William and Mary — 117

A Global Outlook — 123
- Mexico — 125
- Margarita — 127
- The Silversmith — 134

Vietnam — 143
- Trini — 145
- Auntie — 150
- Uncle — 156
- The Police Chief — 159
- The Lord of the Alley — 164

Sicily — 170
- The Crusaders and the Kingdom of Heaven — 172
- The Crusaders' Wives — 176
- The Gypsies (The Roma) — 180
- The Blacksmith — 186
- The Sweet Sicilian Lady — 190

Montserrat, Spain	**195**
Amsterdam	**200**
India	**208**
The Orphan	210
Close To Home	**219**
Peter Branch	221
Jimmy Sparrer	227
Arnold Hudgins	232
A Medical Update	**237**
The Peace Grid	**245**
The End	**250**
Credits (Photos and Graphic)	**253**
About the Author	**255**

PREFACE

I have to admit that I have a tattoo—a physical, forever tattoo—courtesy of Mother Nature. It was caused when a bomb cyclone picked me up and face-planted me on an asphalt parking lot.

My trauma tattoo (the medical label) is on the bridge of my nose.

I coined the term *Soul Tattoos* to describe the unforgettable, indelible marks—inked by *mortals* and time stamped by *milestones*—imprinted on us mentally and spiritually.

Each of the stories in *Soul Tattoos* is about someone or something that has left a permanent mark on me on the deepest level. These tattoos are invisible to the naked eye; otherwise, I would look like a circus attraction, covered from head to toe, inside and out.

We begin life as a blank canvas that is later embellished with permanent reminders of memorable individuals and meaningful moments in our lives. We wear these tattoos as marks of distinction. We have no choice; they have become part of us.

In *Soul Tattoos,* I share with you significant individuals and episodes that have had a powerful and lasting impact on me. Perhaps they will remind you of your own Soul Tattoos.

>Fran Walsh Ward
>Hampton, Virginia
>November 2020

INTRODUCTION

Flashback: Jumping off a cliff. Fast forward: Sitting in a wheelchair.

There is no connection; I do not live a linear life—it's rather a spiraling dance of people, places, and things swirling around in overlap, interconnection, and repetition—with random bursts of the unexpected.

The astrologer said I didn't get one of those lives where everything flows smoothly. It didn't require a mystic to make that observation.

A concurrent view of my past, present, and future is my reality. I have known some interesting people and had adventures and opportunities along the way. I'll tell you about them.

The stories in this book are about people who have been models of behavior by being themselves. They have had a hand in shaping me into who I have become. I begin with the first steps.

I have also shared memories of events and happenings that have made a lasting impression on me.

Fran Walsh Ward

It is with gratitude and joy that I reminisce about these mortals and milestones, for they have left their indelible mark on my heart.

I call them my *Soul Tattoos*.

HOME

"Where Thou art, —that—is home."
—Emily Dickinson

(An American poet who left school as a teen and became reclusive, she was unrecognized in her own time but is known posthumously for her innovative poetry.)

"Acceptance, tolerance, bravery, compassion. These are the things my mom taught me."

—Cynthia Germanotta

(Lady Gaga)

Ma

"Every step you take toward the top is possible because of all the little steps you took in the past. You can climb the mountain, but do it slowly, slowly."

—Dragos Bratasanu

(Author and Space Scientist who empowers Living in Truth, Following Your Heart, and Making Your Dreams a Reality anywhere no matter where you start.)

MA

Baby Steps

"Take baby steps, Francie!" The command sounds gentle and firm. I'm a year old, and I understand the gravity of my mission.

The big people at the kitchen table are watching me. My mother bends down, hands me a whiskey glass, pours milk into it, and says, "Go to Nana." The drama unfolds. My bedridden grandmother in the next room reaches out her hand to me.

I focus on the glass and walk step-by-baby step. I succeed as a First-Class courier. She takes the glass and, thanking me, says (in Lithuanian), "Francie, my four-leaf clover."

A person's first memory is a snapshot of his or her life, a blueprint. We are not prisoners of our pasts; our pasts shape us into who we want to become. My life has been one of performance art and service.

I go back to my first memory because it is the first instance I recollect of being myself. We don't choose the childhood we were given, but we can choose what to do with our childhood memories. What is your first memory?

My friend Ali remembers looking at the glass doorknobs in her grandmother's house. Ali is now a renowned glass artist and owner of a glass studio and gallery.

My first memory expresses my essence. I immerse myself in the moment, giving it my full attention. I am a doer, aware of participating in an event that others might enjoy vicariously. I become engrossed in my activities that others might appreciate. I live a life of service.

My remembrance is one vignette in a sampler of life works as an observer and the observed. The people I have met have distinguished themselves, making an indelible mark on who I am. My mother was the first and most formidable and influential person in my life.

By keeping an open mind and an open heart, we can experience and interact with individuals from whom we learn by example. It is my hope and my philosophy that by being ourselves, living our lives, and letting our lights shine, we light the way for others to have the courage to be themselves so they can shine their lights. We are all in this together.

DAD

> "Let us never negotiate out of fear. But let us never fear to negotiate."
>
> —John F. Kennedy

DAD

The Diplomat

As a child, I would swing on the front gate, pretending to be playing and pretending I was not paying any attention to Dad and the neighbor. Nothing could have been further from the truth. I hung on to every word as tightly as I hung on to the pointed pickets. I did not interrupt, and I stayed until the conversation ended.

We didn't have a phone when I was growing up in Cambridge, Massachusetts; most of our neighbors didn't, either. Contact was made in a neighborly way: in person. Elm Street was a melting pot street. The tenant on the third floor of our house was from Lithuania. The family next door was Portuguese. There were also Italians, Russians, and immigrants from other countries in houses along the one-way street, which stretched two blocks, all the way from Cambridge Street to Hampshire Street.

People kept to their own ethnic mix usually, but sometimes there would be cross-communication. Language barriers needed to be broken down. Cultural values would sometimes clash. That's where Dad came in.

My brothers or I would run upstairs and say someone was asking for Jim. Dad would walk downstairs, and then along the little brick path to the wooden gate at the sidewalk. Dad and the neighbor would shake hands. After a comment on the weather, Dad and I were all ears. I tried to be invisible so I wouldn't be asked to "go upstairs and help your mother." I didn't want to be dismissed. This was big! I wasn't even in first grade yet, but I could tell this was important.

The conversation would go on. Dad, always composed, could defuse a neighbor who had been ready to ignite. Negotiations would proceed until an acceptable solution was suggested, there would be a closing handshake, and the men would go their separate ways.

Dad's best friend was Tip O'Neil. I named my first cat Tippy as a tribute to the longest-serving Speaker of the House of Representatives. I learned about elections at an early age. I handed out pamphlets at the polls for Tip. Since then, I have voted in every election I could. I even changed my voter registration prior to a move to Florida. I serve as an election official, and so does my older brother, Jim. We learned early on of the importance of participating in the electoral process.

Both Tip and Dad were respected men of influence on different scales. Dad worked hard as a meat cutter at Walsh's Market, which he owned with his father, who was from County Cork, Ireland. Grampa had made his way on his own during the Potato Famine. He had been released from his large family and was desperate to relieve them. He arrived in America via Nova Scotia. My earliest recollection of him is when he worked with Dad at Walsh's Market, a meat store. Dad always emphasized the point that it was not a butcher shop. Dad later worked in the meat department of a grocery store chain. He worked in a cold room there, and it took a toll on his health. Although Grampa lived to the age of ninety-nine and shoveled coal for the stove until his last day, Dad succumbed to pneumonia and passed away too soon. It is my honor to uphold his legacy of fairness and justice.

ANUFRA (UNCLE FRANK)

"Appearances are often Deceiving."

—Aesop

ANUFRA (UNCLE FRANK)

> "Float like a butterfly, sting like a bee." -Muhammed Ali

Is it real or is it fake? People have grappled with its authenticity for decades, but it really doesn't matter. Fans love and defend professional wrestling, where performance, entertainment, and athletic prowess mix and mingle with the theatrical. It's a combat sport with a long history. Wrestlers have been found in cave drawings dating as far back as 3,000 BC.

In Greco-Roman wrestling, the oldest competitive sport in the world, competitors use only their arms and upper bodies to attack and hold down those parts of their opponents. Freestyle is a more open form in which wrestlers also use their legs and may hold opponents above or below the waist.

"Introducing, in the red corner, hailing from Brookline, Massachusetts, a freestyle fighter who stands at six feet two, weighs in at two hundred pounds, has a record of twenty wins and two losses, and has ten wins by knockout. He's the current, reigning, and defending champion. It's 'Fighting Frank the Good' Goodelunis!"

The crowd went wild. He was the favorite, at least for that night. Next time, in another arena, under a different assumed name hailing from a different assumed location, Frank might not have been the favorite. It all seems to have been pre-arranged.

Uncle Frank's names included a fistful of pseudonyms that varied depending on the neighborhood ring, the rival, and which immigrant faction he was representing or opposing—Russian, Lithuanian, Polish, or any other.

Uncle Frank wore many hats and satin capes. He spent much time in the ring, as his battered face attested. But I never saw him in the ring.

I saw him in the flower gardens as a master horticulturist who was acknowledged and respected for his garden labyrinth designs and prolifically blooming flowers.

He terrified me as a child, not intentionally, but by his appearance. He had cauliflower ears, a misshapen nose, and scars. He limped when he walked, toes pointing outward, leaving a chevron footprint trail.

He liked me and often patted my head when he could reach me, but I always cowered behind my mother's skirts or ran to avoid him. I was curious about him, though, so I watched his every move, nonetheless. He let me watch him.

"*Anufra*" probably meant Uncle Frank in Lithuanian, which he and my mother used to speak with each other. Was there a connection between his probable first name (Francis) and mine (Frances)?

For my mother, every Sunday he filled an empty mayonnaise jar with water. He put sticks in the jar. I often wondered why Ma wanted sticks to put on her mother's grave, which we visited every week for years. The sticks, of course, were flowering branches from the estate flower gardens, borders, and labyrinths he designed, planted, and tended. We would walk from shrub to shrub until he had collected the branches that met with my mother's approval.

Visiting those gardens made Sundays fun for us. We were free to run and play on the spacious estate grounds, a well-kept private park in Brookline, Massachusetts. Once the jar was loaded in front, at my mother's feet, my brothers and I would race to claim a seat by a window in the backseat of the Hudson.

After arriving at the cemetery, we would say a prayer, then play hide-and-seek around the trees, tombstones, and mausoleums while we waited for my mother, who was in no hurry to return home.

Family was always most important in my mother's mind, and it received her full attention.

Devoted to family, she found herself (along with my father) in the original sandwich generation, lovingly sandwiched between caring for parents and children.

She found time to be present for the living family unit and respectful to those who had passed.

I have always been a fan of pugilistic sports, wrestling, and real or embellished ringside attractions where opponents "Get Ready to Rumble." I find it amazing that grown individuals consent to be subjected to a whomping and, likewise, find competitors prepared to receive one.

I think of Anufra often and imagine him in my corner. I am a Peace advocate, but that does not mean I'm not a fighter. I fight for what's right, but I don't use fists or subject anyone to bodily harm. I imagine that Anufra defends and supports my position. I take comfort knowing that although we didn't talk with each other, we communicated respect and admiration. I look up to him, knowing his occupation in the ring was one of necessity. As an immigrant, he had to find work to support his family. Family has deep roots and can flower under the most amazing circumstances if it receives proper care and tending.

SCHOOL DAYS

"Love the children first, and then teach them."

—Saint Mother Theodore Guerin

(Born in France in 1798 and died in the United States in 1856, A missionary teacher and healer in the Indiana wilderness. A strong leader and an even stronger woman of faith.)

SISTER PATRICIA

"Get thee to a nunnery, go. Farewell...To a nunnery, go, and quickly too."

—Shakespeare

Hamlet, Act III, Scene 1

SISTER PATRICIA

One Door Closes

First grade must have been an adjustment for me. Everything seemed foreign because it was! My brothers and I attended Immaculate Conception School, which was on the first floor of a building where stairs led up to Immaculate Conception Church. The priests, nuns, and congregation spoke Lithuanian, which my mother and grandmother spoke. We attended both the church and the school and complied with singing the Lithuanian national anthem on our birthdays.

School was not difficult academically; I could handle readin', writin', and 'rithmetic just fine. I received a big education that went beyond the basics taught in a standard classroom. I learned to speak my mind, to speak up so I could be heard, and to have people listen to me.

The first example I remember of this education transpired during a parent-teacher conference. My mother, Sister Patricia, and I stood at my desk. Sister Patricia spoke to my mother as if I were not there, saying, "She's too short!"

I am soft-spoken, but as the middle child between two brothers, I have often had to make myself heard, so I said, "No! I'm not! Both my feet touch the ground."

Perhaps my self-righteous outspokenness awoke a mission in Sister Patricia. She chastised me frequently in an attempt to silence my responses. I now realize I might have sounded sassy, but what I said was delivered in childhood innocence.

I never understood why Sister Patricia would make me walk to the front of the room, open my mouth, and receive a coating of hot red pepper flakes on my tongue. I didn't use bad words.

I now attribute my love of spicy food to Sister Patricia, as she trained my palate over the course of that year in first grade.

I was not the only student subjected to Sister Patricia's teaching techniques. All of the black boards were painted green one time. One huge handprint marred the top of an otherwise perfectly color-treated slate. The handprint was obviously made by a big person, maybe even a seventh or eighth grader. When nobody in class owned up to leaving that mark on the board, Sister Patricia whacked everyone with her ruler with the metal edge. I think a show of flesh-colored hands would have been proof enough to vindicate all first graders.

Whacking us did not make the print on the board vanish.

SOUL TATTOOS

On another occasion, Sister Patricia locked me in the closet for playing tag with the boys at recess. Having two brothers, playing tag was natural for me. My lack of understanding that boys and girls were not to play together landed me in the closet—closed and locked. I didn't know how long I'd be there. I didn't want to stay there overnight. I paid attention to what was going on in the classroom. I participated by calling out answers from the dark while standing amidst coats and shelves of books and chalk. I sang and danced during quiet times so I wouldn't be forgotten.

When I was released, I told my mother what had happened. Later, I walked with my mother to the convent so I could apologize to Sister Patricia and so my mother could present the nuns with a homemade strawberry and whipped cream pie.

I didn't know what I was apologizing for, so the next day I told Sister Patricia that the next time she wanted one of my mother's pies, she could just ask me.

There's a show on television that provides a whole education on style through fashion examples. One picture is worth a thousand words. We can learn from negative examples as well as from positive ones, —not to emulate the negative, but so we know what NOT to do.

In child development, the most crucial milestones occur by the age of seven. Children can conclude deep meaning from information that surrounds them. I learned from Sister Patricia, as they say in India, *"What to do and what to don't do."*

MR. DELANEY

"Whether you think you can, or you think you can't,— you're right."
—Henry Ford

(An American industrialist and business magnate, founder of the Ford Motor Company, and chief developer of the assembly line technique of mass production. He was determined to build a simple, reliable, and affordable car, a car the average American worker could afford. Out of this determination came the Model T and the assembly line, two innovations that revolutionized American society and molded the world we live in today.)

MR. DELANEY

Another Door Opens

Though they were only one mile apart, Immaculate Conception School (for a fabled Country Mouse) and Cambridge High and Latin School (for a City Mouse) felt like worlds apart. I played both roles in this fable of my life.

I'm a chameleon. I fit in anywhere. I'm not saying I look like a local—I usually don't—but I adapt to my surroundings. As soon as I arrive somewhere, I'm home. I feel comfortable. When someone in a foreign country asks me for directions, I am pleased. I know I've done it again. I wasn't aware of camouflage as a skill at the time, but I acknowledge now that it is a gift and my superpower.

After switching from a class of twelve in a four-room parochial school on the bottom floor of a Lithuanian church to a public school complex, where my graduating class had 555, I entered a new world, where everything and everyone was different from the old country.

I started out slowly. Having attendance taken in homeroom, deciphering my schedule, finding my rooms, learning teachers' requirements, and summoning courage to talk to other students filled my plate that first day.

I picked up speed after a week. The classes were all too easy. I heard about Honors classes. I wanted in!

I went to the Dean's office. Mr. Delaney was imposing, but he did not seem as intimidating as the nuns. I explained my wishes to be in Honors Math and Honors English. He asked, "Where's your mother?"

I answered, "She's at home. She already graduated from high school." I listened as he lectured me about being respectful, but like my playing with the boys at recess, I didn't know what I had said that was offensive. It was with pride that my mother spoke of high school. In our neighborhood at that time, graduating was a degree of accomplishment.

It was explained to me that everyone in the Honors classes had been students together for years at Peabody School in North Cambridge. I was from East Cambridge.

Request denied. I visited those Honors classrooms after school and during study hall. I asked the teachers to test me and ask a few questions. I persisted. The students eventually stood up to the teachers for me, and the teachers finally stood up to Mr. Delaney for me, who consented on a trial basis. I never looked back.

SOUL TATTOOS

When I returned textbooks to my first week teachers, they were disappointed that I was "dropping out". I wasn't. I was moving forward. They said I showed promise. I was pleased to have received my first words of encouragement in a new world.

MR. BURNS

"Tell me and I forget, teach me and I remember, involve me and I learn."

—Benjamin Franklin

MR. BURNS

No Do-Overs

High school English class. Do you remember yours? Mine was just another class. I was just another student. Nothing was unusual. Everything was run-of-the-mill. So why can one class—and why does one teacher—become so memorable? We often don't know when someone has become an influence. It is fortunate when we do.

Mr. Burns did not let me get away with something. Why is that memorable? I was a really good student. I did my work well. I devoted a lot of time to studying. I was the original geek, walking a mile to school while carrying an overload of books in case I needed something. I always carried my violin. I was prepared.

Except there was one day I had to forego an English homework assignment in order to study for a physics test.

"Pop quiz!" The very sound strikes fear into the hearts of college-bound seniors. We were to write, from memory, Shakespeare's Speech: "Friends, Romans, countrymen…" as spoken by Marc Antony.

SOUL TATTOOS

I could not recall a word of it, since I had not committed the speech to memory. I received an F for my quiz score. *"No problem. I'll memorize it during study hall next period,"* I thought. I memorized it during study hall and returned to Mr. Burns's class to retake the quiz.

"No." There were no do-overs. I couldn't believe it. I had a perfectly good excuse for why I hadn't memorized it the night before. I had done all of my homework every day up until then. I was contrite, and I expected leniency. But I was out of luck. Mr. Burns stood like a rock, unyielding. His red wavy hair and tweed jacket remained unruffled. I did not.

There were several lessons I learned through my folly of expecting things to go my way:

- "If things are not going my way" is my definition of ego.
- I am not the center of the universe.
- Timing is everything.
- I am responsible for the choices I make.
- There is an effect to every cause.

I carried over Mr. Burns's standards and applied his techniques to my own teacher's bag of tricks when I taught high school English.

One class of seniors mutinied and chose not to do the reading assignment (read chapter one of Herman Melville's tale of a whale.)

I gave a pop quiz. No one could answer even one question. Everyone had a perfectly good excuse. They had to study for a chemistry test. I understood and was sympathetic, but I was also unyielding, and I wrote a column of red zeroes in my grade book.

The class hated me. I hoped they would take Mr. Burns's lesson to heart and learn from it as I had. They asked if they could read it that night. Of course, and the next chapter, too.

The next day, they were ready for a quiz. There was no quiz. Oh, another thing I learned: Life is not fair.

THE PROM

"A gentleman is one who puts more into the world than he takes out."

—George Bernard Shaw

(Irish comic dramatist, literary critic, and winner of the Nobel Prize in Literature for *Pygmalion*.)

THE PROM

VICTOR LEVOSHKO

"Will you go to the prom with me?" Victor asked.

On the very first day of school, that question set off my senior year with a bang, not a whimper.

Despite many other concerns, the two deepest causes of handwringing on this senior girl's mind were twofold: about the prom—who would ask me and what would I wear? The intrigue and wonder for my year were squashed by Victor Levoshko on Day One.

"Yes, I will," I answered him, but I felt deflated. His invitation took all of the fun out of it. Mystery was replaced with a foregone conclusion. I am not a person who will accept an offer and then change my mind if a better offer comes along. I keep my word. The word to Victor was *yes*. I was locked into what had been anticipation of a dream that instantly morphed into my fate; it was set in concrete.

Fran Walsh Ward

A nice guy, Victor was blond and had Slavic good looks. He wore glasses and dressed conservatively, usually in chinos and a sport shirt. My mother liked him. He was *that* nice. My mother wanted me to marry "a nice Lithuanian boy". Victor's Russian pedigree came acceptably close to meeting her requirement. Bearing my mother's seal of approval provided good enough reason for Victor *not* to be on my list of desired prom dates.

Many a senior girl envied me, however, because I had already clinched a prom date. I was the only one who didn't seem ecstatic. Life is strange, and high school girls are even stranger.

The anticipation of wrapping up high school had many classic, universal facets. Taking college board exams—plus the daily stress of keeping grades up—was scary enough for any senior, but I had additional stressors of running against a rival in student class elections, and working after school and on weekends. Pressure loomed large.

Senior year proceeded at Cambridge High and Latin. Victor and I hardly knew each other, and we did not become much closer as the year progressed. He did invite me out for my first date ever, then took me to see the latest movie the first week it was showing, which included the opening scene of Julie Andrews singing on a hilltop.

We went to a theater in Boston that was across the river from Cambridge. We had an awkward drive to the theater as we tried to break the ice. We didn't seem to have much in common that we could discuss. In the theater, an attempt at holding hands was fumbled. At sixteen, navigating social skills as part of growing up is a challenge. Some pick up the skills easier than others.

Victor, however, seemed to know the rules that the rest of us were trying hard to decipher, and he attempted them bravely.

John Valerio, on the other hand, was a person who tried hard but who hadn't understood society's rules. A few missteps landed him in Swansea. The name of the city was synonymous with reform school. No one (not enrolled there) knew that that meant the residents of the therapeutic boarding school spent their days being *re-formed* into demonstrating more mainstream behaviors than what came naturally to them.

Somehow, somewhere in Cambridge during senior year, I met John Valerio, a shy, tall, dark, and handsome Greaser with a cool attitude like James Dean's, complete with movie star looks and a black leather jacket. One day, I invited John home for a cup of hot chocolate. My mother made the cocoa, served it to us, and joined us at the kitchen table for a polite, reserved conversation. Following John's departure, my mother pronounced that I could no longer be associated with John, whom I had already determined to be the love of my life. The reason for his being exiled: he had been in prison.

"What did you say, Ma?"

"Only people who have been in prison drink from a cup by holding it with both hands."

How did she know this ersatz fact? Truth was immaterial. My mother had decreed it, branding him for life. Henceforth, I never mentioned John again in her presence. I never invited him home again.

Young love thrives. I accepted his black leather jacket as a badge of our passionate affection for each other. I continued to stash it under the stairs and would retrieve it and put it on when I was beyond the sight of my mother's watchful eyes at her vantage point at the second floor living room window. I wore my sign of fidelity (John's Rat Pack jacket) both to school and on the way home, then removed it before I rounded the corner and turned from Cambridge Street onto Elm Street. Wearing the distinctive words and the drawing of a rat in white served as suitable consolation for John's being exiled from my house.

Secretly, away from family's eyes, I met John daily at Harvard Square. I juggled my part-time after-school work at Harvard to be able to maintain my social connections with friends and classmates.

When prom time approached, my mother coordinated my look. Always in charge, she sewed a really pretty, long, fitted dress for me. The white empire lacy bodice topped the skirt of heavier yellow fabric. She treated it as an artwork with pretty lines that went unmarred by the bulk of a zipper. Without a zipper, the chastity dress denied easy access.

Prom day arrived. I had waist-length red hair, and my mother directed the beauty parlor on the corner to pin it up into a then-fashionable beehive hairdo. Squirming into the dress was the only solution. My mother wrapped my high updo, and my head, in a plastic dry-cleaning bag.

She wriggled the dress onto me as I stood in Superman position, arms up. Once my head ejected through the neck hole, I ripped the bag off of my face, gasping for air, but at least I was in!

Victor drove to the house and came upstairs for obligatory pictures in front of the living room drapes. We drove away as all of the neighbors who had been awaiting my appearance watched and waved. We drove two blocks. Victor stopped the car and opened my door. He shook hands with John, who had been waiting nearby, and drove away as John led me to his motorcycle. I put on a helmet, then hitched up my long, tight mermaid gown, freeing my right leg to swing over the back of the bike. I held on to John's waist casually, and we zipped through traffic, weaving in and out of lanes, riding to the prom in style. We waited our turn for parking, in line with both cars and limousines.

Inside, we danced to the music of the day, the song of the year by Sam The Sham & Pharaohs, and plenty of songs from The British Invasion, including music by The Beatles, The Rolling Stones, and Herman's Hermits. Besides that, we heard songs from our domestic shores, including music by The Beach Boys, The Temptations, The Righteous Brothers, and The Supremes. Capping the night off was Sonny & Cher's theme song.

We danced all night, had our picture taken, and returned to Victor's waiting car hours later, after the prom had ended. Victor held the car door open for me, and John drove away, waving. Victor walked me upstairs to say goodnight to my family and me.

I could only suggest to my mother that gravity and doing the Bunny Hop had slithered the beehive hairdo from the top of my head onto my forehead, looking more like an alien growth. Who would have suspected that the cause was a motorcycle helmet?

My hero, Victor, understood social skills, friendship, and maybe even love. During our fiftieth high school reunion, I wanted to thank Victor. It was Victor who had conceived the plan for me to attend the prom with John. I wouldn't break my word, but Victor had asked me what I wanted and honored my wishes.

SOUL TATTOOS

I found out that Victor had died, but his memory lives. His name was on the memorial table for lost classmates, but it didn't state the circumstances of how he passed. Victor was the kindest, most unselfish gentleman. E. E. Cummings is probably the school's most notable graduate, but Victor Levoshko is probably the most honorable sixteen-year-old ever to have attended Cambridge High and Latin School.

THE ARTS and SCIENCES

"The most beautiful thing we can experience is the mysterious. It is the source of all true art and science."

—Albert Einstein

HARVARD and MIT

"When you think about Boston, Harvard and M.I.T. are the brains of the city, and its soul might be Faneuil Hall or the State House or the Old Church. But I think the pulsing, pounding heart of Boston is Fenway Park."

—John Towner Williams

(Greatest film score composer of all time.)

HARVARD AND MIT

Following Directions

My father wanted me to go to Radcliffe, but I wanted to go to Harvard. They weren't open to female students yet, but where there's a will, there's a way. Harvard University is devoted to excellence in teaching, learning, research, to developing leaders who make a difference globally. They are also committed to community service. They offered practice-teaching opportunities to their students who are aiming to be teachers. Those potential teachers needed students. I have taken two courses from Harvard's brilliant students: one taught music theory, and one taught Russian language. I have applied what they taught me many times since.

High school college-preparatory classes at Cambridge High and Latin were challenging enough, but when the opportunity to enrich my education appeared, I added the extra activity of working after school at Harvard for seventy-five cents an hour. This may have been one of the first situations where I applied my rule of saying yes to the universe. Harvard needed students part-time in the Physics and Psychology Departments. I applied. I was hired, and I began to change my perspective. Literally.

My first assignment was in the Psychology Department; it was a behavioral study. I was given a pair of prism eyeglasses. As soon as I put them on, I felt woozy. I was dizzy and couldn't see straight. My vision had been perverted. I had to hold on to walls and practice walking with distorted eyesight. My balance and depth perception were gone. I clung to handrails and slid my feet carefully, inch-by-inch, to ascend and descend stairs. It took me longer than my usual twenty minutes to walk the mile home along Cambridge Street. I wore the glasses for a week during my waking hours, which included at school, to the amusement of classmates who teased me as mercilessly as I would have taunted them.

Finally, the day came for the glasses to be returned. I learned that you have to be careful what you ask for. I had looked forward (again literally) to normal vision. But I learned that there was going to be another learning curve: this time, I had to learn to become accustomed to walking without prism glasses and a return to prior normalcy. I had to relearn balance and depth perception. I had to hold on to hand railings and slide my feet carefully, step-by-step, to ascend and descend stairs. I had finally learned to walk home in twenty minutes during the week I wore prism glasses, and it was now taking longer than twenty minutes as I adjusted to wearing no glasses for a week. After I finally completed the behavioral study to the satisfaction of the psychologists, I learned that things aren't always what they appear to be. Sometimes factors, internal or external, can distort our vision.

My next assignment was with the Physics Department. I tested textbooks that professors had written. I followed the instructions, as they were written, to conduct the experiments. I seemed to be the guinea pig, but it was the professors who wrote the books who were really the ones being tested. It was their instructions that were under the microscope. The professors were present as I executed the experiments. "Do it right!" they yelled. "Do you want me to follow the directions as written?" "Yes." "That's what I did." The men, neither technical writers nor authors, needed instruction themselves on how to write instructions to perform a task. Arranging points in logical, sequential order is essential, and it proved to be their weakness. The problems that needed to be solved were of the egos of the brilliant physicists. They wanted me to achieve their envisioned results though they hadn't provided instructions that would yield that outcome. It was a bitter pill for them to swallow.

I loved that project, especially following directions implicitly and eliciting the irate exasperation of the professors. I learned that experts may not necessarily be perfect.

SOUL TATTOOS

I learned that humility and humor can set many things aright.

With my first paycheck, I bought a Samsonite briefcase at the Harvard Coop. When I went to the University of Massachusetts as a freshman, I carried that briefcase proudly. It was part of my uniform—briefcase, white go-go boots, and a polka-dotted mini-skirt. Students thought I was a foreign exchange student.

I carried the lesson of that physics job to my writing classes, especially with middle schoolers. I advise students to Dress for Mess. The homework assignment is: Write instructions for constructing a peanut butter and jelly sandwich. The next day, I provide materials, and each student eats the sandwich made from his own instructions. Student A reads his directions aloud in class that he had written, and student B follows them precisely as student A reads them. Audience participation and aha! moments are plentiful.

There is a lesson in writing what someone means and in meaning what someone writes.

My home was midway between Harvard and MIT (Massachusetts Institute of Technology), which is ranked number one in the World's Top one hundred Universities. (Harvard is ranked number three.) I took my first computer class at MIT, where we used punch cards and binary code, learned the computer languages MAD and FAP, and walked by rooms filled with massive machinery, including the computers, which had to be debugged periodically in RAID-insecticide style.

The Harvard professors I worked for wrote recommendations for me. As a result, I secured part-time work at MIT in the psychology department. I was trained to use an electron microscope to count DNA in monkey cerebellum. Exposed to great thinkers, I was at MIT during an exciting time. My classmate David's father, Jerome Lettvin (in MIT's electrical, bioengineering, and communications physiology departments) had debated Timothy Leary on the merits of LSD. More importantly, Dr. Lettvin conducted a study that proved toilet paper should be placed on the roller in the over position. He knew so much about everything. He would have been a great game show contestant of Alex Trebek's. He loved forceful disagreements and unshrinking opponents. He loved ideas and debating them. He had wanted to be a poet, but his mother had ordained that he should be a doctor, so he studied medicine. He said, "I was fortunate enough to have had a father who was an anarchist. He pointed out to me that the interesting things always lie out of the beaten path. You look for them, and when you find them, you play with them.'' I like his style, which I also espouse.

I value the time I spent with the esteemed professors and brilliant minds at Harvard and MIT. They always found time to give me, an interested student, explanations in a new field of study. I was fortunate to have known these learned men. They were great teachers, and they were great people, for shining their lights to show me the way.

THE ISABELLA STEWART GARDNER MUSEUM

"In our life, there is a single color, as on an artist's palette, which provides the meaning of life and art. It is the color of love."

—Marc Chagall

(Belorussian-born French painter, printmaker, and designer who composed his images based on emotional and poetic associations, rather than on rules of pictorial logic.)

THE ISABELLA STEWART GARDNER MUSEUM

Art and Beauty

I own every major museum in the world. At least, that's how I *feel* whenever I enter any one. Of course, I do not own the property rights or the artistic properties within. I am not responsible for dusting the collections, insuring them, or guarding them.

Intellectually and emotionally, however, they are mine—all mine. I am grateful to everyone responsible for sharing and show-casing the masterpieces, the gifts of beauty, and the thought-provoking creations from time immemorial to the present and into the future.

When I was ten years old, my mother introduced me to each of the museums in Cambridge and Boston. The Peabody, the Agassiz, and the Natural History Museums at Harvard housed exhibits of Archaeology, Ethnology, and the glass flowers, which were one of the Seven Wonders of the World at the time. My favorite museums housed art collections. After my mother's introductory tour series, I was free every Saturday to visit any museum of my choosing...solo. I lived in them. I loved them. I did my homework in them. Having carte blanche entry to galleries and music venues, I adopted an innate sense of ownership.

I grew up in a student-friendly environment—admission to cultural sites was free in Cambridge and Boston and $1 for opera or BSO (Boston Symphony Orchestra) dress rehearsals. MIT and Harvard were an academic and intellectual playground. I am self-educated in art and music; I never took cultural electives in school—I was too busy studying *important subjects* like physics—but I could not help but learn to love both science and the arts in my own backyard.

I combined my love of the arts and sciences at The Isabella Stewart Gardner Museum. Located near Fenway Park (where I frequently sat in the bleachers to cheer on the Red Sox), the Venetian Palazzo is a personal display of architectural splendor from antiquity. It has European masterpieces and stunning formal gardens. I sat on a marble capital in the courtyard, under a Byzantine arch, using my slide rule for calculating physics homework problems, while admiring the palms and colorful courtyard garden, and smelling the dreamy orchids and fragrant fruit tree blossoms.

I rewarded myself for finishing my work each day by wandering through the immersive environments of art, architecture, flowers, plants, and textiles.

I love Isabella Stewart Gardner's collections and her emotional approach. Exhibits are not labeled conventionally, as they are in nearby MFA (Museum of Fine Arts, Boston). Isabella (she and I are on a first-name basis) wants visitors to find their own meanings—an inductive approach, which I prefer. She generously built her museum "for the enjoyment of the public forever".

I was the high school girl who appeared daily, then vanished by closing. Twenty years later, however, when I returned for a visit, a guard took my hand in both of his and said, "Welcome home, dear!" They had always known me and welcomed me home. I had considered myself invisible, but my Love of Beauty had not gone unnoticed.

I knew what I liked. Art opened my eyes, and it opened my mind. I would spend hours at the Museum of Fine Arts. I loved the classics. I hated modern art. Then one day, I visited the Fogg Museum of Art at Harvard. There was an exhibition of huge works by Noland, Stella, and Louis. I made it a point to memorize their names; I knew it was an important day. No one can change anyone else's mind, but you can change your own mind, and that's what I did. I loved this work. I started loving modern art for the first time and forever. I could still love the classics; while, paradoxically, loving another concept, too. I knew then that I could be flexible and open-minded and that I could have two conflicting thoughts at the same time. I was aware that it was my first conscious paradigm shift.

Little did I know that my self-taught arts education would initiate my love of the arts and clarify my view of life. Everyone has a common denominator for making sense of the world. For some, it's music; for others, it's movies, a certain cuisine, or football. For me, it is a love of the arts—the various branches of creative activity, such as painting, music, literature, and dance— *appreciated primarily for their beauty or emotional power.*

I had rheumatic fever when I was a child. I read Dean Ornish's book about transforming one's own heart. The book discusses the concept and practice of meditation as good for the heart. I went to a free introductory meditation class at the Edgar Casey Center in Virginia Beach (A.R.E). We were told to close our eyes, and, that appearing on the screens of our closed eyelids, there would be a word that would be the guiding principle of our lives. A word appeared! It was BEAUTY. I was so disappointed. I thought that my word was a shallow concept. (I was thinking of beauty pageants, which I do watch as religiously as I watch award shows. They're a barometer of our culture and mores.) It was not until years later that I realized that Truth and Beauty are jackpot words.

Beauty is the guiding principle of my life. True beauty is defined as the state of *being authentic and sincere in a way that extends love to yourself and others. It feels real, safe, alive, playful, flowing, authentic, and life-giving.*

SWEET SIXTEEN

"A mind that is stretched by new experiences can never go back to its old dimensions."

—Oliver Wendell Holmes, Jr.

(Among the most famous of the U.S. Supreme Court justices. Known for his "clear and present danger" argument about the limitation of free speech.)

SWEET SIXTEEN

Work-Study

My sixteenth Spring, Dad asked me what my plans were for the summer before my senior year of high school. I answered blithely, "I think I'll read."

He said, "No. You'll work." Welcome to reality. Where would I work? What would I do? Those questions could wait for answers. Dad took me to the Social Security office for my social security card. My younger brother came along for his, too.

I liked to read, so I went job hunting at a few libraries. I liked Hayden Memorial Library at MIT (it's an iconic image), so I started there. I went back every day to see if they would hire me that day. I don't know if they appreciated my persistence or if I beat them down, but I was hired to work at the Reserve Desk on the graveyard shift, which was eleven p.m. to seven a.m. As I stamped book cards, I met students who were nocturnal. If someone asked me out, it would be for a breakfast date before I walked home two miles to sleep during the daytime. So much for a leisurely summer! But I met some fascinating people and had my hand on a lot of books that introduced me to a broad range of topics.

My mother decided I should be an optometrist. She said it was clean work to examine eyes and fit glasses, and they have Wednesdays off. Since I didn't have a better idea, I applied at the Massachusetts College of Optometry in Boston. I was the first female who had ever applied. I was accepted. I only needed one year of pre-med somewhere first.

That sounded easy enough, until my mother informed me they weren't paying for my education. That didn't rattle me, either. I figured I would work my way through pre-med. I had already proven to be a reliable worker.

When I was accepted at the University of Massachusetts, I signed up for as many classes as I could to get my money's worth! My parents would not fill out the form saying I was independent and paying my own tuition. If they had declared that, I could have received a scholarship.

So I used my tried and true formula for applying for a job. I went to the Reserve Desk in the library at UMass every day until they hired me...for the graveyard shift. I could handle that. But this time, I didn't have the luxury of sleeping after work. I had six classes to attend, and I had to study, write papers, and take tests. I couldn't do all of that every day.

SOUL TATTOOS

Some people were understanding. I didn't tell anyone about my situation, but they noticed that I wasn't always in class and alerted me that there would be a test in some class the next day. I stayed afloat. One professor in particular, made an impression. Since daytime was my nighttime, I would be in class, but often ended up sleeping in class. The physics professor, who wore train overalls and a railroad hat, would walk up to me in the large auditorium and blow the train whistle in my ear. After several repeat performances, the students turned on him. No longer amused, they felt compassion.

Somehow, I got through Freshman year, but being a female in pre-med at that time was met with opposition. The times they were a'-changin', but not fast enough for me.

In vertebrate zoology, students had to capture their own critters for dissection. Sadly, I was the biggest game hunter, and I trapped the most moles and varmints with peanut butter and oatmeal bait. The day we had to *wade* shoulder-deep in the Connecticut River to net fish with our bare hands was my Waterloo. Hip boots were distributed all around, except to me. They were for the men. I couldn't swim despite having taken lessons for years. I wanted to. I can't swear that anyone tried to kill me that day, but my resolve to complete the pre-med program was killed, and I gave up the Doctor of Optometry idea. I had never capitulated before. I was receiving quite an education at this school.

I continued my studies in English literature, which required no ensnaring of small animals or wet field trips, only dry reading. I decided to become a teacher and educate others through formal means *and* through my own experiences.

HIGHER EDUCATION

"For the things we have to learn before we can do them, we learn by doing them."

—Aristotle

DARTMOUTH COLLEGE

"I learned that courage was not the absence of fear, but the triumph over it. The brave man is not he who does not feel afraid, but he who conquers that fear."

—Nelson Mandela

(South African activist and former president who helped bring an end to apartheid. His message was one of peace, justice, and freedom.)

DARTMOUTH COLLEGE

Jumping into the Unknown

I started this book with a flashback of jumping off a cliff. I didn't elaborate then. I will now. When the mountaineering instructor said, "Jump!" I jumped.

That was in Hanover, New Hampshire, at Dartmouth College.

A Dartmouth education is exceptional. Person-to-person teaching and opportunities for creativity and applying knowledge foster a love of learning in its students, empowering them for a lifetime of leadership, locally and worldwide.

Dartmouth provides lifetime education, excellent academic programs, personal attention from top faculty, opportunities to participate in research, and a close-knit community. (A member of the Ivy League, Dartmouth has been educating leaders since 1769.)

My journey in graduate education began at Dartmouth and continued in the same vein as the pre-med program at UMass. I was entering another male bastion. I was in the first class of female graduate students. Just because women had finally been admitted academically, however, did not mean we were *accepted* into the boys' club. I stayed in my lane. I knew I had to work harder, play harder, and do everything better in order to shed my cloak of invisibility. Acceptance was unattainable. Success was defined as not being scorned by the men. I was not seeking recognition. I wanted equal access to the promises of the mission statement.

I did receive recognition, however, earning citations with my master's degree in science and my master's degree in mythology. Always working to pay for my education, I worked on the botany rooftop greenhouse, where my job was to feed and water the subjects (angel wing begonias) for the Plants and Human Affairs course. I had yet another experience with an electron microscope (as I did at MIT). I watched the lifeblood of the plants flow through the veins in the leaves. It was awe-inspiring. This time, In the mythology department, when Professor Tatum suggested I pursue a doctoral degree in mythology, I was reminded of my early high school days, when the teacher said I showed promise. I followed the advice of the learned professor, not in mythology, but with a PhD in metaphysics. They are closely linked.

My most stellar accomplishment at Dartmouth was earning the respect of my male counterparts—in the classroom and in the wild.

SOUL TATTOOS

I am a guinea pig. I always go first, whatever the challenge. I have learned that if I lag behind because I'm trying to master every detail by watching everyone before me, I still might not get it right. If I go first, using my understanding of correct procedures, I finish before obsessing about how to start.

Rappelling is the most dangerous—and frightening—part of climbing. I joined the Dartmouth Outing Club to take advantage of Dartmouth's location on the Appalachian Trail in the White Mountains. I had climbed four-thousand-foot peaks, summer and winter, but I had never rappelled. This was an opportunity for empowerment. I did not have fancy equipment, but I was given a harness, a helmet, and instructions. Everyone was fearful of jumping off the cliff. I volunteered to go first. If I could do it, they had to! It was a matter of honor. (In this book there's a picture of me scaling the cliff I jumped from.) They could not let a woman show them up. We all reached the bottom safely. There were congratulations all around.

I loved the Dartmouth Outing Club. I climbed mountains with the members, rappelled off cliffs, and canoed down white-water rapids, though I couldn't swim. The greatest lesson I learned at Dartmouth: SHOW NO FEAR! NEVER LET THEM SEE YOU SWEAT!

MY NEW WORLD

"The future belongs to those who believe in the beauty of their dreams."

–Eleanor Roosevelt

THE LOG CABIN

"The greatest fine art of the future will be the making of a comfortable living from a small piece of land."

—Abraham Lincoln

THE LOG CABIN

Survival and My First Teaching Job

It takes ten cauldrons of snow (and eight hours) to make one cauldron of water over an open fire. My main task one day during a blizzard was to convert snow into drinking water. I hoped I had enough firewood inside to achieve my goal and to last through the numbing night.

I had nailed a tarp to the logs that were inside, lined along one wall, to prevent snow from blowing in between the logs where the chinking had broken away. The expression "blanket of snow," was an accurate description in the log cabin. When I woke up that morning in my sleeping bag, I was covered by Nature's duvet.

The wind howled, but the dogs howled louder. I opened the cabin door, holding it tightly so the wind wouldn't rip it off its hinges. Three dogs bounded through the deep snow and into the cabin. They shook and splattered snow and wet dog spray as they vied for a warm spot in front of the fireplace. The room lost heat from when I opened the door and was introduced to three chilled critters, but I had to give them shelter.

They probably needed more food, but I shared what I had. I stoked the fire, piled on a few logs, patted the dogs again, watched them curl up together for warmth, tucked myself into my sleeping bag, and bawled like a baby when I heard the dogs lapping up the entire cauldron of water—my whole day's survival effort.

I was exhausted, hungry, thirsty, cold, and miserable. I was alive.

Morning came with bright sunshine, a new attitude, and a new day. I opened the door, and the dogs raced out, each step in the snow deeper than their height. They were on their way, continuing on their path from the previous night, along Hogback Ridge in The Plains, Virginia.

I took one step and was thigh-deep in snow. The snow was so deep, it was laborious walking; I was getting nowhere, slowly. I was looking for the chicken house. I couldn't see it. I was standing on top of it!

Most of the year, I enjoyed living in the simple log cabin. My nearest human neighbors were three miles away. Companionship was provided by black Angus cattle that were grazing, and along with the woodland creatures—wild turkey, hawks, and eagles, and various varmints. I loved to shout, "Hey, groundhogs!" and watch dozens pop their heads up from their burrows, like a live game of Whack-A-Mole in the fields.

I cheered for the fox that raced by. It was followed by the Middleburg Hunt, which started with sniffing, running, baying foxhounds, then followed by the hunters and jumpers, ridden by traditionally-attired men and women of the Middleburg Hunt (in scarlet outfits with apple-green collars and brass buttons that had the initials MH). There would be no kill that day, but that would not deter the liveried Hunt Breakfast.

I was a recluse on the mountaintop, but I drove my Datsun pickup truck every day to The Hill School, a country day school where I taught fifth graders basics and extras. What a wonderfully exciting experience we all had then and there. A crowning achievement was directing *Antigone* by Sophocles in the most-moving production. There were no dry eyes in the auditorium.

There is ample opportunity for people-watching everywhere in the world, and I found opportunities—whether I was far from home or in an old-fashioned general store on The Plains Road, on my way home to the log cabin. While I was waiting my turn, the little bearded man said, pointing to a shelf, "Let me have a jar of "them pickle. I forgot about pickle. It's been a long time I had one." He was polite, endearing, and memorable.

I had visitors often. Among the most memorable were my two friends who were returning from serving in the Peace Corps. They said they hadn't eaten anything but cassava in whatever country they were in (that has probably changed its name several times now.) Everything I served was simple and appreciated. Dessert came with déjà vu, as they said they had forgotten about strawberries. It had been so long since they had had them.

My cousin Philip visited upon his return from Russia, where he had worked in a State Department position. As soon as I arrived home, he said he had to leave. He said he had never been as afraid as he was after parking his car at the base of the mountain, climbing/hiking up the rocky, rutted road, and running across the fields. I asked why he ran. He said he hadn't known if out-running a bear or climbing a tree would be better. I asked why he would do either. He said that even in Russia, he had never seen so many bear tracks. I said I hadn't seen or heard of any bears. He pointed to the field covered with the "bear tracks" he was referring to. He thought the steaming mounds were bear poop. What he had seen were cow pies, "meadow muffins," fertilizer left behind, courtesy of the black Angus.

Humor is everywhere in the cosmos, even in a log cabin.

THE WHITE HOUSE

"...I Pray Heaven to Bestow the Best of Blessings on This House and All that shall hereafter inhabit it. May none but Honest and Wise Men ever rule under this Roof."

—John Adams

(At the insistence of Franklin Roosevelt, the quotation was inscribed on the fireplace of the State Dining Room immediately below the portrait of Abraham Lincoln, which was done.)

THE WHITE HOUSE

The People's House

"Put the gun away!" I shrieked.

"You have to have a gun when you're driving in Washington," he countered. I didn't know that; I never did, but he worked in the district, and the driver makes the rules.

He was driving too fast and recklessly from my point of view. He changed lanes, rounded corners, and took big risks with my life. He turned off the street and into the driveway, and then casually raised a hand out his opened window. The guard at the booth nodded and smiled. Tires squealing, he made a sharp right and screeched to a halt. Good thing I had my seatbelt on. He said, "Come on. It's okay. I work here."

"You'd better go in and check," the schoolteacher in me advised cautiously. I waited in the Volkswagen as he took the steps, several at a time, and entered the building that had been named by President Theodore Roosevelt.

Grinning from ear to ear, my host returned, waving for me to join him. Bowing with a flourish, he announced, "Welcome to The White House!"

SOUL TATTOOS

"Are you sure I'm allowed in?"

He replied authoritatively, "The White House belongs to all citizens of the United States."

He held the door open for me. What followed was a tour rivaling that which any dignitary has ever received. My insider's look was not the official guided tour, but it was better, as I saw highlights of the 132 rooms, thirty-five bathrooms, and six levels of the "President's House" and "Executive Mansion."

We had the place to ourselves. Occasionally, I would see a guard (one of my host's co-workers) peering at us. As we entered rooms along the corridor, my guide flicked on light switches.

The first room we entered was the Lincoln bedroom, which included President Abraham Lincoln's office and Cabinet Room. I was breathing the rarefied air of President Lincoln's private space (with a huge bed that he did not sleep in) and office (if he had slept in the room, it was probably at his desk). The room is best known for being a guest room used by presidents to reward friends and political supporters.

I expressed my surprise that John James Audubon, the world's most famous artist of birds, was holding a rifle in his portrait, and my host responded, "How do you think he got those birds to stand still so he could paint them?" I hadn't thought of that. (I read later that to become knowledgeable, the self-taught naturalist-painter had killed and stuffed thousands of birds.)

Back in the corridor, sumptuous aromas were emanating from a doorway. We went in the pantry and found racks of delicate pastries. I was given one. *I have dined in the White House.*

Then we danced. In what might have been a ballroom, we waltzed across the large room and exited. I was shown fabulous furniture pieces in the corridor, such as a Chippendale desk with secret compartments. Each piece of furniture had a story and unexpected features.

Before entering the Oval Office, one of the most powerful places on Earth, I was instructed not to sit on any furniture. The room was monitored twenty-four-hours a day. Surveillance was not as sophisticated as it is now. According to my host, if anyone were to rise from a chair before the President (then Nixon), it was treated as an act of aggression, and a guard would enter, prepared to shoot. I didn't know how much of what I was told was truth or exaggeration. Anything is possible.

It was also possible that Henry Kissinger, former United States Secretary of State and National Security Advisor, was both an idealist and a realist. We entered his office next. His "shuttle diplomacy" (flying back and forth between Middle Eastern capitals for months) was an effort to bring about peace after the 1973 Arab-Israeli War.

SOUL TATTOOS

That evening, there was a half-eaten sandwich on his desk. Artwork across from his desk was a large oil painting of unrestrained boldness in shades of red and black—not what I would have expected, not something to evoke a feeling of Peace.

We went to some storage rooms on a lower level. They looked like museum galleries with display cabinets. One housed the presidential porcelain china (usually chosen by each President's First Lady).

In one room, there were magnificent gifts that had been presented to the Presidents. If a gift was unsolicited and valued at $20 or less, the President (or any member of the Executive Branch) could keep it. Otherwise, it was accepted, catalogued, and stored. A white marble replica of the Taj Mahal, for instance, covering a huge table, is the property of America and Americans, and not the presidential recipient. The room was a hodgepodge, like a fantastic, mythical attic.

Walking down a corridor, we reached a staircase, and I was invited to go upstairs in the "President's Palace" to watch President Nixon sleep. I declined.

At the foot of the stairs were two paintings draped with black fabric that covered the subject matter. The official portrait of First Lady Jacqueline Bouvier Kennedy was to be unveiled the next day!

I had to see it! It took my breath away; it was so beautiful! I couldn't take my eyes off the oil-on-canvas portrait. It was ephemeral, soft, magical. It was Camelot.

I knew I could describe it and write about it. I had a scoop for *The Washington Post*! I could also get my friend fired, though.

Little did I know then that three paintings (of Jackie Kennedy, of Audubon, and in Kissinger's office) would have such an impact on my life. I had never written about artworks before, but I was inspired. Since then, I have written countless art reviews for artists, for individuals, exhibitions, galleries, and museums. I have had several art columns in magazines and newspapers.

Departing The White House by sunrise, we returned to our friends' wedding reception looking like Cheshire cats. That was some enchanted evening!

THE FOXCROFT STUDENT

"When the Student Is Ready, the Teacher Will Appear."

—attributed to Buddha

THE FOXCROFT STUDENT

Role Reversal

I learned an important lesson while I was a teacher. Education is a two-way street. Teacher and student are interchangeable roles.

I once drove one of my geometry students at Foxcroft to town for coffee in town at The Coach Stop in Middleburg, a town halfway between Washington, D.C. and Winchester, Virginia. During colonial times, a coach would have stopped in this area so passengers could stretch their legs on their several-hour journey.

Foxcroft is a girls' boarding school in Middleburg with many multi-national students. This one particular girl was originally from Canada, but her family was living in Dubai at the time; her father was with ARAMCO (the Arabian-American Oil Company). Our backgrounds and our homelands were worlds apart.

After coffee, we went window-shopping and entered some high-end stores. Shopkeepers welcomed the polite Foxcroft girls and their deep pockets. We went into an antiques shop/art gallery that was full of contemporary and classical art from far away, in both time and space.

SOUL TATTOOS

Everything we saw was beautiful! I admired a stunning portrait of a horse, painted with a backdrop of scenic nineteenth-century England.

The next day, she surprised me with a gift: the painting I loved. Gasping, I said, "It's exquisite! It's precious! It's outrageously expensive!"

Crestfallen, she asked me, "Isn't it good enough for you?" "Oh, yes! It's too good! I couldn't accept it. It's too much!"

I handed it back to her. "I can't accept such a gift. It's too dear! It's worth the equivalent of several years' rent for me." I was applying my standards and values, not hers.

I don't know if she returned the painting or whatever happened to it. The next day, she gave me something she said she knew I could accept. A Gucci scarf. Yikes! In comparison to the painting, this must have been like a dollar-store trinket to her. The day before, I would have said I couldn't accept that! I hugged her and thanked her even though I knew that that was too expensive, too. I realized that when someone gives a gift, it is important—first of all—to accept it graciously. By accepting the gift, we show our appreciation, whatever its monetary value. When we accept the gift, we accept the *giver*. By accepting a gift, we validate the giver and show we accept the honor of being appreciated, for that is the spirit of every gift ever given. The *thing* is something; the *message* is everything.

I have learned my lesson. I have accepted *everything* given to me ever since. It had always been easier and more important for me to give than to receive, but I realized I was doing myself—and others—a disservice by not allowing people to give to me, by my refusing the pure motive and expression of their love for me.

I am grateful to that worldly student. She gave me a gift of understanding.

THE GOLF TEAM

"Golf is the closest game to the game we call life. You get bad breaks from good shots; you get good breaks from bad shots, but you have to play the ball where it lies."

—Bobby Jones

(A great man and the model of the complete golfer: —supremely gifted, of vast intelligence, and of profound character.)

THE GOLF TEAM

Strength of Character

The old joke is that the word GOLF is an acronym for Gentlemen Only Ladies Forbidden. That's not true now, and it mostly wasn't true when I moved from northern Virginia to teach at Hampton Roads Academy. In an independent school, teachers are asked to fill roles as they are needed. They needed a Varsity Boys Golf coach. I didn't play golf, but I accepted the challenge. Since most of the players already knew how to play, my role was in uniting the students as a team. They were strong individuals, and they became a team of force and distinction. I assigned practice three days a week. On the honor system, they chose their own days and locations—solo, in pairs, or in groups. Some days I would drive a carload of players to play at Fort Eustis Military Base or at the public golf course, and then for three hours I'd walk the course in the three-inch heels I wore in the classroom. I would crisscross the course, walking a few holes with each player, one-by-one.

I learned so much from the golf team. I certainly learned about golf, about the sport (form, technique, and strategy). I also learned about each individual (interests, outlook, and matters of importance).

Golf is a psychological game. I could advise about a swing, but the greater success was in our many discussions of abstractions.

Self-confidence was one. Everyone's dreaded shot on one course was from a bluff overlooking a pond before the next green. The players all took out beaten-up golfballs with smiles and dings because they expected them to become gator bait. Without explanation, I asked for a new ball fresh from a sleeve (a box of four). No one wanted to sacrifice one to me, but someone did. I asked for someone to hand me a club. Someone handed me something. I teed up the ball…swung… the ball soared over the water…and landed near the pin! It's all about confidence. Could I duplicate that shot? Probably not in a million years, but the one time I needed to make a point, I nailed it. They all took out new balls and fired away. Every ball landed on the green.

As for ladies being forbidden, the golfers accepted me. It was the coaches from the competing teams who objected to a female coach. "On what grounds?" I asked, but there was no answer to my face.

When it came tine for the golf matches, I selected the six players who had shown the most promise during practice that week. I watched them play under pressure and heard their descriptions hole-by-hole when they finished their rounds.

SOUL TATTOOS

Each and every one of them possessed a strong code of ethics, a sense of self, pride of accomplishment, and teamwork. They made observations of others, teams and individuals, and drew conclusions. The team did not hold back with each other, and they were equally analytical of their opponents. Golf pencils are three inches long and have no eraser. The players took out their cards and pencils from their pockets after each hole and wrote down how many shots they took. They compared notes and challenged a discrepancy. The golfers had amazing visual memories and knew where each ball went—their own and those of their opponents.

After a match they would reveal to me that certain opponents had falsified their scores. It was a data point. The behavior and morals of the individual golfers reflected on their schools. The teammates during matches were ambassadors of Hampton Roads Academy. They would agree with Tiger Woods, that in Golf, decency and honesty matter more than achievement.

The competitors would question each other not only about scores but also about values. It was a diverse group, including one girl, one black player, and one Jewish member. The country club they chose for practice one day did not admit blacks or Jews as members. There was a heated discussion in school that day. Some students did not know of the restrictions in the club where their families had held memberships all their lives. The team, in solidarity, chose to practice at the public golf course. Arnold Palmer believed that strength of mind and character were greater factors of success than strength of body. The empathy the team portrayed opened a dialogue that extended beyond the Golf Team as sportsmen to the Student Body about sportsmanship.

The other coaches acknowledged that Hampton Roads Academy's undefeated 9-0 season was exceptional, despite my being their coach. The team players are still outstanding individuals, on and off the golf course, continuing to make a mark in their chosen fields of endeavor and in life.

THE COLLEGE of WILLIAM and MARY

"We can easily forgive a child who is afraid of the dark; the real tragedy of life is when men are afraid of the light."

—Plato

THE COLLEGE OF WILLIAM AND MARY

The Ivory Tower

The leading industry in Massachusetts is higher education. I grew up in a rarified atmosphere of academia—"the ivory tower"—a metaphorical place where people are happily cut off from the rest of the world in favor of intellectual pursuits, disconnected from the practical concerns of everyday life. I wanted to be a dean.

Continuing the graduate education I started at Dartmouth, I enrolled at the College of William and Mary in the Higher Education Administration Department with my eye on the prize.

I was a graduate student working as a graduate assistant to various professors. I was proceeding along my path, but things started to smell fishy. I worked for a William and Mary professor and a visiting professor from Rutgers. I enjoyed supervising student teachers who were practice-teaching in local Williamsburg schools. I was pleased to write for the two professors. I was surprised that they took full credit in their books for my ideas, conclusions, and writing. I was not wearing a cloak of invisibility, yet. I was sequestered, introduced as "my graduate assistant" but not as their ghost writer. I was getting an inside look behind the scenes.

An opportunity presented itself. I applied for and was instated as Associate Director of Financial Aid. It was a powerful position that included faculty status. My office overlooked the Sunken Garden. I was in charge of distributing $9,000,000 of federal, state, local, and institutional funds annually. There were protocols, forms, and formulas to be followed, respected, and verified. Decisions for distribution of funds were not taken lightly. Financial assistance could take the form of grants (money given with no strings attached), loans (to be repaid), and work-study (local jobs in restaurants and school libraries; students must work to receive their pay/financial assistance). Usually, aid was a complicated combination of all three.

I would not bow to the demands of certain department heads and give funds to their offspring who did not qualify.

Financial aid has changed over the years. Being smart does not usually qualify a student; being poverty-stricken might. There are complex factors based on data provided on a student's application.

I announced that I was not going to be interviewed on *Sixty Minutes* and that I was not going to serve time for violating federal laws by distributing funds to individuals who did not meet the criteria for those awards. There were deserving students who met the guidelines, but funds had been depleted.

I was told I was part of the "Ol' Boy" network" now, and that I would do as they said.

My ivory tower was crumbling. It was like learning too much about Santa or the Easter Bunny. I could not and would not violate the ethics of the position. I had been placed in charge of moneys, and I honored the trust that had been bestowed upon me.

I had conversations with the men who had made the demands. I was not mistaken. They were serious. So was I. I reported them to the upper echelon. I went to the President of the College and to the Head of Human Resources.

No one ever followed up with me. They all knew about it and were in on it. I went to the Dean, whom I had always looked up to. He said he did not believe me.

I resigned from my position. Several times, I was offered a raise and a promotion to stay on. I declined.

There were repercussions for upholding my principles. Retribution came in the form of punishing me academically by requiring me to cultivate a new doctoral committee. This meant starting over from scratch. I had already begun my doctoral dissertation of "Personality Traits of College Presidents' Wives. I would have used a personality inventory that identifies a person as being in one of sixteen distinct categories of psychological types. It could have become a popularized study.

I had sampled the ivory tower, and it was not for me. I picked up my life and took it in another direction.

I immersed myself in a PhD program in Metaphysics.

I have no regrets. I have no regrets about anything in my life. I gather the facts, make the best decision I can at the time, and don't look back.

A few years after that William and Mary chapter in my life, I read a newspaper article that said the Dean had been walking home after dark, had spotted a fire in a dormitory, and had acted quickly. No one was hurt, and the building was saved. I wrote to the Dean to congratulate him on his quick thinking, and I said his halo had slipped when I had reported the dark financial aid episode to him. He said he couldn't say anything to me at the time, but that he knew he should have done things differently. Yes. I agree. I know I did the right thing.

A GLOBAL OUTLOOK

"The best and most beautiful things in the world cannot be seen or even touched—they must be felt with the heart."

—Helen Keller

(American author and political activist, the first deaf-blind person to earn a Bachelor of Arts degree, she changed the lives of millions of people with visual impairments, bringing them courage and hope.)

MEXICO

"Those who don't believe in magic will never find it."

—Roald Dahl

(Spy, ace fighter pilot, chocolate historian, and medical inventor. Author of *Charlie and the Chocolate Factory* and *Matilda*.)

MARGARITA

"The greatest good you can do for another is not just to share your riches but to reveal to him his own."

—Benjamin Disraeli

(The Victorian prime minister.)

MARGARITA

Street Smart

Sometimes we get more than we bargained for. That's what I got when I won an auction item: a week's stay at a house in Taxco, Mexico. I invited my brothers and their wives, and we enjoyed the first vacation together we ever had in our lives.

Everything was new to all of us. The setting was exotic, with picturesque homes and surrounding mountainous landscapes. The language was foreign to our ears (this was my first international experience). It was a wonderful adventure.

The house came with the services of Margarita. She was about four feet six and was feisty. Margarita spoke no English. We spoke no Spanish. It was a match made in heaven. Our communication consisted of Margarita's shouting at us louder and louder until we nodded that we agreed with her, not understanding what we were agreeing with. I kept muttering phonetic pronunciations from my Berlitz book and pointing out words to her on the pages. I finally caught on that although she pretended, she couldn't read. But, boy, could she ever communicate!

Fran Walsh Ward

When Margarita walked in the house with bags of groceries, I wanted to know where she had bought them, as I hadn't seen a grocery store anywhere. We finally got through a marathon conversation via charades and hand-flapping; (we both stuck with it). The reward was that I accompanied Margarita to the market the next day.

I have always loved marketplaces. Growing up, we used to go to the market in South Boston every Saturday night in the summertime. I used to think the market was a blast, and this one proved to be just as much fun. One of the first indoor/outdoor markets in Mexico, this one could be approached off the main walkway in Taxco by walking down steep stone steps that seemed almost as old and primitive as the pyramids. There, not visible from the street I had walked down several times, was an open market. The steps themselves along the sides had many stalls with produce, along with a number of open-front bakeries, some making and selling rolls called bolillos (Mexico's favorite white bread), others making tortillas. Some made desserts. Each shop specialized. My sense of smell was assaulted with all of the sweet and yeasty smells emanating from ancient stone ovens. My sense of sight was overjoyed by the colorful clothing worn by the throng of men, women, and children heading upstairs or downstairs. The hubbub along the stairs sounded thunderous—rich, full, and talkative—but any meaning from the Spanish language was as elusive and alien to me as separating and identifying the blended aromas.

SOUL TATTOOS

Another set of steps descended into another, lower level of the market. Here, it was colder. Even though we were there at about 7:00 a.m., the heat was already almost too much. Downstairs, though, it was naturally air-conditioned and enclosed in the earth. There were closely packed booths and stalls. Space was at a premium and was efficiently utilized. Resources were displayed simply and elegantly.

I went to the market each day with Margarita and learned more each day. She was a master of communication. Especially since I didn't know the language, what I learned from her was through observing her body language (her different postures, with hands on hips), her tone of voice (from sincere to sarcastic), her volume (from whispering and secretive to bold and scolding), her hand and arm gestures (from waving hello to dismissing a product or person), the comical rolling of her eyes, the expressions of emotion (from heartfelt to maudlin), and the complex human interactions she had with those she chose to acknowledge.

Margarita was different with each vendor. With some women, there was a simple and easy camaraderie. An easy banter and chit-chat completed the transaction. Some were good friends; gossip must have been the specialty at that booth. I was all ears. Little good it would do me; unless it was my brothers or me, I didn't know anyone Margarita was talking about.

One woman Margarita treated rudely—both visibly and verbally. I was surprised at the venom in her voice, and by the fact that Margarita traded with her at all. She must have had a monopoly on the cascarones, the eggshells filled with confetti, which Margarita bought for my brother's birthday.

My favorite interaction of Margarita's was one where she seemed genuine and without façade. It was as if this merchant was the only one who could see through to the real Margarita, and she allowed it. The bean seller was blind. He was a tall, dignified, white-haired man who wore a grey business suit with no shirt underneath, but there was a white handkerchief knotted around his neck—kind of a Chippendale look! He had the most organized and precise display at the market. Wooden boxes lined with plastic were stacked, to reveal beans of different colors, sizes, and types. They rested on a board on a slant. The scale had the glass removed, so his hand could feel the indicator, and he could tell the weight as he rested a bag of beans in the holder that was swinging from the gauge. He was a gentle man. Margarita ordered her beans, and she did not assist him and do it to her liking, as she had with all of the other merchants. She waited patiently and almost reverently as he filled the small paper bags with whatever she requested. She did not fill the air with chatter; she sat on a folding chair quietly, like a little girl on her best behavior in response to his paternalism. I was observing something special during that encounter, but I will never know what.

Margarita went from stall to stall purposefully. She would call hello as she passed by on her way to the next stop. She would flirt with a merchant, chide a salesperson, intimidate, tease, cajole, beg, bargain, or berate. She was a graduate course in human relations, business, finance, time management, and psychology. I don't know what Margarita thought of herself, but I had a good idea of what others thought of her, as I saw the looks in the eyes of the people who had just sold her goods. She commanded respect.

Margarita was more than a cook and a housekeeper. I wonder how many others she had mentored. I imagine that someone under her wing who could communicate in the same spoken language could be educated and trained to become a dynamo, applying Margarita's self-taught skills.

I am fortunate to have accompanied Margarita to this marketplace, with parallels to remind me of that marketplace from my childhood. Both places were filled with moments for people-watching, learning, native culture, and fond memories.

THE SILVERSMITH

"The richness of silver is immortal. It doesn't die."

—Antonio Pineda

(Perhaps the gentleman in the Taxco shop.)

(Internationally renowned Mexican modernist silversmith who was praised for his bold, striking jewelry designs and ingenious use of gemstones.)

THE SILVERSMITH

The Seduction of Silver

There was no magic involved. It was only an experience. But any experience in Mexico seems magical.

It was after a siesta and before dinner. I walked to the Zocalo, the town square in Taxco, where everyone assembled for the same reasons: to pass the time and watch the sunset. I meandered along the streets, browsing in the shop windows. I had always walked on by the jewelry shops; but this time a window display caught my eye, and I took a second look. One particular necklace was strikingly unusual. Like all the other jewelry, it was handcrafted of silver; but this one had an elegant appeal, albeit a primitive feel. I wanted to see more. I opened the door and walked down the steps to see if there were similar pieces. I was greeted by a gentleman who introduced himself graciously. I told him my name, and I told him of my joy in viewing the work in the window, and of my intention to admire similar craftsmanship. I also told him I would not be purchasing anything; the jewelry was too rich for me. He laughed and poured a glass of sherry for me, over my objection. He wanted me to stay as long as I liked and to admire anything. He was flattered.

The shop was like a museum. The works were all different: whereas some seemed like classic, ageless pieces, some were ultra-modern. They were mostly made of shiny silver; some were made of gold, and many had hand-polished stones or gold coins. Some patrons in the shop were especially intrigued by the gold coin collection. Dark-eyed, exotic saleswomen were wrapping purchases for their clientele. While they spoke to their customers, their eyes followed us. The shopkeeper accompanied me around the shop, bringing me from one showcase to another. He allowed me to hold the exquisite works, and he placed some around my neck or on my fingers to show how they were meant to be admired more fully. I commented on his salesmanship abilities, but he shook his head and said he did not know how to sell. He hoped he could learn how to craft. I asked him if he had made anything in the shop, and he said he had. All of it. I did not believe he had much left to learn.

He asked if I wanted to see his favorites, and; of course I did. We did not go unobserved on our way to his office. We walked to the back of the shop and down a few stairs, where he opened the door for me to enter. He walked to one wall, swung a painting hinged on one side, and opened the safe. I would have laughed about the theatrics of the situation, but my heart was pounding too hard. When he pulled open the door of the safe, I could feel a heaviness in the room. The lighting had not changed, but the temperature must have dropped.

I felt chills along my spine. He took out a leather pouch and said that what was in it was "especial". He asked if I still wanted to see, as it would change my life. I told him that I had already felt that my life was changing. I loved an adventure. He nodded and said he understood. We sat at his worktable, which was covered with jewelers' lenses, tools, and bits and pieces of treasures in the making. He cleared a place as he cleared his throat and spread out a piece of black velvet. He spoke with difficulty, slowly and swallowing often. I was beginning to feel frightened and told him so. He said that that was as it should be. I stopped him before he proceeded. I wanted to know if he showed whatever was in the pouch to all who entered his shop. He looked me in the eye and said that I had already known the answer before I asked the question. He said, "Do not doubt yourself."

Finally, amidst the charged atmosphere in the room, he gently shook a marble-sized stone into his other palm. He placed it on the cloth. We both lost our breath. He said he did not know much about it. It was found in the Aztec burial grounds at the site of the chieftain's grave. I asked him how he happened to have it, as it is illegal to buy or sell antiquities in Mexico.

While I waited for his answer, I picked up the carved head of shiny black stone and felt overcome with a strange sensation that I still cannot identify. I was aware of nothing yet everything. I could hear the hum of voices in the shop, yet that seemed like trivial background noise compared to the sound of the waves and the wind.

SOUL TATTOOS

I put the stone down and thought, "Waves?" We were at least a hundred miles inland and at least a mile high in the mountains of the silver region.

When his voice interrupted my thoughts, it was a different voice. Or I heard it differently. He said that his grandfather had given it to him, and it had also been given to his grandfather. I asked who gave it to his grandfather, and he said he had also wanted to know. His grandfather told him that when they had both died and were butterflies and were free, that they would both understand. Until then, there were some things that could not be expressed. The jeweler returned the stone to the pouch and put it in my hands, which he cupped together between his. He leaned over and brushed first one cheek and then the other with light kisses. Butterfly kisses. He said that someday I would understand. I protested and said I could not keep anything so precious. He said he knew that. That someday, I would give it away to the person who would know.

I walked to dinner on legs made of Jell-O; and Margarita, the housekeeper, watched me but did not ask questions. The strange is commonplace in Mexico.

The Taxco vacation behind me, I took the chicken bus to Mexico City for my flight home. I enjoyed the sights and sounds, if not the smells. The goat, pig, baby, and orange peel aromas were identifiable. I did not know if it was the old man, his burlap sacks, or the iguana on his shoulder that added another wave of tang to my nostrils.

Once, in Mexico (the natives refer to the city as Mexico as we natives refer to our city as New York), I was killing time in a 5&10, reading the Easter cards in Spanish and doing some last-minute people-watching. I passed by the postcard section and stopped to take a look. The back of a card with the Aztec calendar said that the original is housed in the National Archaeological Museum in Mexico City. It was 4:30. I ran out of the store and asked the first person walking by where the museum was located. Between my broken Spanish and her patience, I learned it was far down the street I was on, but she said that a bus went that way every hour. I had to see the calendar. I hailed a cab and found the entrance to the museum. 4:47. It was still open. I had to get inside before they closed.

But I was stopped by a man who kept calling, "California! California!" I looked back to see what all the shouting was about. He was shouting to me. I said he had the wrong person. He asked if I wasn't from California where was I from? He repeated, "Veer-gee'-nee- uh!" I was racing up the steps; he was racing as fast as I was. He asked if he could show me the museum. I thanked him but said I only wanted to see one thing. I bought my ticket, had it punched, and walked through the turnstile. "Veer-gee'-nee-uh!" Oh, no. He was calling from behind me, and then he was at my left elbow, guiding me to the Aztec calendar while providing a monologue that was good-natured and informed. I calmed down after I saw the exhibit from every angle; and then he said, "Now I will show you what you came to see." I told him I had come to see the Aztec calendar, and he nodded his head and smiled. We walked past exhibits of pyramids, stones for grinding corn, and then a glass showcase that was by itself within a room of fountains and unusual lighting. The feeling was different—no longer like a museum, but like a church. He stretched out his hand toward the exhibit; I looked at him questioningly, then bent down to look. The label read, *"From the tomb of Moctezuma, the last Aztec emperor of Mexico."* There was the stone the jeweler had given me! It was as if I had had the wind knocked out of me. I turned to my jolly, self-appointed tour director. He was gone.

There was no magic involved. It was an experience. But any experience in Mexico seems magical.

The adventure is ended. The memory lingers. The stone remains a treasure, but as the mysterious gentleman had predicted, it is no longer in my possession. There are no coincidences.

VIETNAM

"I can't say what made me fall in love with Vietnam— that a woman's voice can drug you; that everything is so intense. The colors, the taste, even the rain."

—Graham Greene

(British author who wrote novels of suspense and moral ambiguity.)

TRINI

"How important it is for us to recognize and celebrate our heroes and she-roes!"

—Maya Angelou

(American author, actress, and civil rights activist best known for her 1969 memoir, *I Know Why the Caged Bird Sings*, which made literary history as the first nonfiction bestseller by an African American woman.)

TRINI

A Hometown Hero

My friend Trini—one lucky Vietnamese refugee—was to be airlifted, in utero, in 1972 during Operation Frequent Wind, the largest helicopter airlift in history. 7,000 were evacuated from Saigon via chopper in under twenty-four hours during the last days of the Vietnam War. As this was happening, at the same time 150,000 North Vietnamese troops were just outside Saigon, ready to pounce.

American Forces Radio broadcasted Bing Crosby's famous Christmas song on the morning of April 29 and announced the "temperature was 105 degrees and rising" —The signal! Americans and hand-picked Vietnamese headed toward predetermined assembly spots.

Air America choppers started the evacuation flights early that morning, with seventeen military and civilian versions of UH-1 Huey helicopters. The original plan called for most flights to arrive and depart from the U.S. Defense Attaché Office, near the airport, but as word of the evacuation spread, thousands of Vietnamese headed to the embassy compound.

Thick crowds jammed the gates, some holding papers that claimed they had worked for the Americans. Others said they were dependents of American citizens. Many feared their U.S. connections would put them in danger under a North Vietnamese regime. Embassy Marine guards chose who to let inside, beyond the chaos and tsunami of people.

Trini's mother, however, would not leave her little daughter, who was reaching up, but had not been added to the helicopter. Her mother jumped down.

Little Linda lived her days indoors, unseen in Bông Són, Bình Dịnh, Vietnam, where Trini was soon born. Linda's head was shaved so she would look like a boy and could escape the terror of the regime wiping out girls.

Trini was born in Bông Són and is an American citizen now living the American dream. (So is Linda Dang, who is an inspiration!) They are enterprising, running their own businesses: nail salons. They employ family members brought over from Vietnam and have employment awaiting them.

Prior to their arrival, Trini has sent financial and emotional support to them.

Trini invited me to visit her family in Vietnam. (We had previously vacationed together in Egypt and Jordan and were good travel companions.) I accepted her offer.

When we arrived in Vietnam, her family—rightfully—hailed her as a hero returning.

SOUL TATTOOS

Her gifts of constant support as well as her ingenuous personality could explain our reception in the five locations we visited in Vietnam. Her sister Thu Thào; and her sister's husband, Cao Khang, their beautiful daughter Thào Vi, and three charming sons (Raymond Khang, Bo Cao, and Cao Day Tien) made me feel so welcomed that I felt like a card-carrying member of the family. I hated to leave.

AUNTIE

"What is there more kindly than the feeling between host and guest?"

—Aeschylus

(A great ancient Greek writer known as 'the father of tragedy'. He believed there was a universal law of justice, an ordinance governing the whole world.)

AUNTIE

Hospitality

I once drove all night across the Bonneville Salt Flats in Utah. The natural feature, where no life forms can exist, resembles an alien landscape. It was formed by the evaporation of an ancient lake; salt and minerals dissolved in the water and were left behind as a solid layer. The Salt Flats are used as a raceway for setting land-speed records. I drove, not to set records, but to dash my Datsun pickup truck to the next point on my cross-country odyssey one summer. The vehicle couldn't have survived crossing during the daytime sun.

It was exactly as Ella Fitzgerald famously sings it! Driving on the unmarked salt flats is at the driver's own risk. There are no road stripes. There is only following and staying with the pack of others crossing. When the Salt Flats are dry, it is safe to drive on them, staying within one hundred yards of the edge of the salt crust.

I survived by consuming more and more water, even though I had been drinking water constantly. I had never been as thirsty in my entire life as I was at the end of my several-hour crossing of the salt flats. I rubbed my arms down with my hands, and flakes of salt cascaded to the ground! My body had evaporated the gallons of water that

SOUL TATTOOS

I had consumed, the same way that the salt flats had been evaporated into existence.

Fast forward to my visit to Vietnam with my friend Trini, who had invited me to visit Vietnam and her extended family. I asked if we should warn them we would be coming to visit them in their homes. She said, "This is Vietnam. Where else would they be?"

We visited her brothers, sisters, half-brothers, half-sisters, cousins, all of their spouses, all of their children, and the extended families. Each stop was its own cause for celebration, festivities, and a visit *home*.

It was a long walk to visit her aunt and uncle one day. We walked one dusty dirt road after another, past houses, through rice fields, and past cemeteries, turning down one road after another, passing little family churches and shrines, smelling incense, and admiring flowers placed on roadside altars, as is Buddhist tradition.

After walking for the longest time, we arrived at a tiny property bordered by tall, lush coconut palm trees that provided shade. The coolness was like magic! We morphed from sweltering, weary walkers into welcomed guests. At this farm, which consisted of a small house, a shed for a pig, the pig, and a pigpen in a yard of ankle-deep dust, everything was dry. Oh, so dry!

Rain is a priceless commodity in the rice fields. The family, though they all lived in different cities, all had a shared experience. They described it like this: Whatever time of day or night, if someone yelled "RAIN!", everyone would race to the fields, fill the waiting empty buckets, and water the crop.

I was parched when we arrived at Trini's aunt and uncle's farm. I never want anyone to go to any trouble for me when I am their guest, but when Trini's aunt asked if we were hungry or thirsty, I said I was really thirsty. My remembrance of the salt flats surfaced.

Trini's diminutive aunt sprang to action. I thought she had chores to do. She went behind the pig shed and retrieved a tall, primitive ladder of bamboo and carried it to a towering coconut palm tree. She climbed steadily to the top and reached up, yanking a coconut from its bunch and tossed it to the ground. It looked like a bowling ball dropping into a dust bowl. Dust clouds arose. Then she fired down two more coconuts, which joined the first one. The sound was a dull thud, and the air was filled with grey grit. She scampered down the ladder and put it back, just as any farmer would return tools and equipment automatically.

She went in the house and came back with a machete.

This delicate little lady held a coconut in one hand and whacked the daylights out of the coconut, scalping it without spilling a drop of precious liquid. She handed the rustic drink to me with the biggest grin! It was the best garden party, and it was with the best drink I have ever had in my life. Now, that's hospitality!

UNCLE

"Forgiveness is the fragrance that the violet sheds on the heel that has crushed it."

—Mark Twain

(American writer lauded as the greatest humorist the United States has produced. William Faulkner called him the father of American literature.)

UNCLE

Forgiveness

Trini's aunt and uncle were so pleased to see Trini, and they welcomed me heartily as a member of the family. The conversational tone was universal and needed no translator. It was full of happy sounds and questions concerning the health of family in America. Trini's uncle was talkative and jolly. He wore a shirt and slacks with the legs folded up. He sat in a wheelchair. He was an amputee. His legs were gone, the result of a war injury. He did not say it was from the Vietnam War. The people don't call it that in Vietnam. They call it *The American War*.

I apologized to Uncle. I said I didn't understand what the war was about. He said, "Nobody does. It's over." He did not hate me or any Americans. He was the most forgiving person. The conversation continued with topics of the present day.

It is easy to see what I learned from Uncle. No matter what, forgive. And let life go on.

THE POLICE CHIEF

"It is the close observation of little things which is the secret of success in business, in art, in science, and in every pursuit of life."

—Samuel Smiles

(Scottish author and government reformer who concluded that more progress would come from new attitudes than from new laws.)

THE POLICE CHIEF

Finding My Vietnamese Voice

Each visit was a gift! The relatives shared whatever they had with us. Dinners would often became parties so friends and neighbors could meet Trini, their American success story, and her American friend. Everyone went to great lengths to make me feel welcomed. I did!

I loved watching the food prep in the kitchen. Usually, the men were the cooks. They used ingredients somewhat familiar to me, but they used fresh items, whereas I was familiar with items of the canned variety, like water chestnuts, bamboo shoots, and coconut milk.

At these gatherings, I did a lot of listening but could not contribute to the conversations.

In one city, though, I had my greatest communication triumph. The police chief, a family friend who had previously lived in the city where Trini grew up, hosted a party for the family in a private Karaoke club. I was an observer. What else could I be? I watched the monitor. At the bottom of the screen were the Vietnamese lyrics of the Vietnamese words, but they were in our recognizable Roman alphabet (of ABCs), which made the words readable and pronounceable for me.

Fran Walsh Ward

At the end of a night of revelry and drinking adult beverages, we all stood in a circle, swaying to the final song while, facing the screen, arms wrapped around each other's shoulders. The police chief caught a glimpse of me singing, did a double take, then suddenly made everyone stop singing. He ran over to me while reaching the microphone out to me. I read and sang the final verse solo! The crowd erupted in applause, hoots, and hollers! It felt good to be one of the gang!

THE LORD of THE ALLEY

"Leadership is something you earn, something you're chosen for. You can't come in yelling, 'I'm your leader!' If it happens, it's because the other guys respect you."

—Ben Roethlisberger

(Pittsburgh Steelers quarterback.)

THE LORD OF THE ALLEY

Innate Ethics

Trini and I left her hometown of Quy Nhon for the metropolis, formerly Saigon, now Ho Chi Minh City (named for the communist revolutionary leader).

I had often heard Saigon called Sin City, but the most frequent crimes against foreigners are petty thefts—purse snatching and pickpocketing. Smartphones are more lucrative targets now. Vietnam is relatively safe, and people obey the rules. When Vietnam introduced Head First, a compulsory national motorcycle helmet rule for all drivers and passengers on all roads, it took only two weeks for complete compliance. Violators had their motorcycles and scooters confiscated. Gulp!

There is both Communist rule and street law. Trini and I stayed at a hostel in Saigon, where friends owned a restaurant nearby. During the daytime, we could walk down the alley that opened up into an open-air market where vendors hawked their colorful and aromatic wares, including fresh fish, homegrown vegetables, sugar cane, and incense. Nighttimes were good times for us to be indoors

SOUL TATTOOS

because of unpredictable nocturnal activity of humans and animals.

We were there long enough to make the acquaintance of a number of street people. I don't know where they lived if it was not in that alley. I never saw bags characteristic of the homeless. Individuals—men, women, and children—would casually lie back on a landing sometimes—or stretch out in the alley—and sleep. No one seemed to be employed, but they always had money.

One man was articulate, not from a formal education, but from the streets. He spoke English and Vietnamese. He was the authority in the alley. Women who worked in the hair and nail salons, as well as derelicts, conferred with him to settle issues.

Trini wanted another piercing in one ear lobe. She went to him. I was aghast and suggested she should wait until we returned home, but she insisted that he do it!

"Get me needles and white thread," he told one alley boy, who ran to the push carts in the market.

This would be the most unhygienic procedure I had ever witnessed. Trini said, "It's okay. Don't worry. I'm not worried." The surgeon du jour licked his fingers, twisted the white thread with those fingers, threaded the needle, then pierced her ear. It didn't even bleed. He pulled the thread through, made a loop, and knotted it.

Trini's friend Cindy said, "I'm next! But I *am* worried." He pierced her ear as she screamed.

Her ear lobe swelled, turned red, and bled. I took her picture at the moment of penetration. She looked like Edvard Munch's model for his famous painting of a man, screaming. Trini said to her, "You didn't believe!"

One alley boy was five years old, too old to be running naked, but he always did. He hovered beside me as I was eating outside at the restaurant once. I offered him food, and he ate it. The owners told me later not to do that again, as they fed him. I asked why no one seemed to take care of him? I had seen him hose himself down in the marketplace with the hose used for cleaning pushcarts and the ground at the end of the day. They said his mother was a drug addict and didn't want to give him up because the government gave her money to support him.

I watched from my third-floor hostel window once as he looked down the alley and then urinated on a stray dog. The dog did not walk away; but it endured the abuse. Later that day, the little boy and four men—the lord of the alley, the restaurant owner, and two high-powered entrepreneurial friends—left the indoor part of the restaurant. The boy was crying; I had never seen him cry previously. I asked, "What's going on?"

"Just having a little talk."

The four men were the boy's disciplinarians. They took it upon themselves to teach him morals and acceptable behaviors. I was so pleased to have met all of those men. Rising to fulfill their own sense of duty and greatness, acting *in loco parentis*, the men provided the boy with guidance and a moral compass. They were trusting the universe, believing that everyone rises to his highest level of competence. It was an act of grace that they were an example of Divine Order.

SICILY

"Going to Sicily is better than going to the moon."

—Gabriel Garcia Marquez

(Writer who gave Voice To Latin America. The master of magic realism was the region's best-known writer.)

THE CRUSADERS and THE KINGDOM of HEAVEN

"Convictions are more dangerous foes of truth than lies."

—Nietzsche

(German philosopher who criticized the view that good is everything that is helpful, and bad is everything that is harmful.)

THE CRUSADERS

(My Heroes)

The Crusaders have always been my heroes. Ridley Scott in his epic historical drama film about the Crusaders echoes a variation of my own battle cry of life in these lines from the movie trailer about The Kingdom of Heaven:

- "Be without fear in the face of your enemies."

- "Safeguard the helpless, even if it leads to your death: that is your oath as a knight."

- "The world will decide what becomes of us. This is a new world, a better world than has ever been seen. There you are not what you were born, but what you have it in yourself to be—a kingdom of conscience: Peace instead of war. Love instead of hate. That is what lies at the end of the Crusade."

- "No matter what you do every day, be a good man. What God desires is what's in your head and in your heart. Our King has no need for a perfect knight. Go to pray for the strength to endure what is to come."

SOUL TATTOOS

Having seen the movie, I vowed to visit Messina, Sicily. I knew that a pilgrimage to the Duomo, the cathedral, was my new crusade. I researched and found a cruise at a reduced rate and recruited friends to share a Mediterranean cruise adventure with me.

The island of Sicily was conquered and settled by Muslim invaders from North Africa in the ninth century and was reconquered by the Normans of southern Italy in the period of 1061-1091. Thereafter, the island and various mainland territories came to form a kingdom that became one of the major powers in the Mediterranean region. Messina, Sicily, is the port from which the Crusaders sailed to the Holy Land.

The much-anticipated day arrived when we docked in Messina. Visitors had various reasons for Messina to be on their personal bucket lists. My friends Marti and Nick went to Palermo to see Mt. Vesuvius; I was inebriated by the scent of the sea and intoxicated by the sight of Tunisia, which was a few scant miles away, across the Strait of Sicily. I headed for the historic area, a tourist destination, to see Orion's grand ornate water fountain and its detailed sculptures, designed by one of Michelangelo's students.

THE CRUSADERS' WIVES

"Pursuing peace means rising above one's own wants, needs, and emotions."

—Benazir Bhutto

(Former Prime Minister of Pakistan.)

THE CRUSADERS WIVES

Loyalty and Sacrifice

After locating the beautiful square of Piazza del Duomo, I entered the Duomo, Messina's Norman-designed Cathedral, which is dedicated to the Madonna. Constructed by a renowned architect from Florence and a protégé of Michelangelo's, it boasts several significant features. In the interior is an impressive polyphonic organ, one of the largest in Europe, still functioning perfectly. The chapel, to the left of the main altar, was sponsored by Crusaders' wives, whose royal portraits grace the murals on the walls. The chapel shows their devotion to the Crusaders, their heroes, as it portrays fervent wishes for them to return home safely. The atmosphere in of the Cathedral of Messina is full of devotion, sacrifice, hope, faith, and love. The wall of individually lit candles glows with impassioned flames of prayer.

In support of their champion Crusaders, there is a strongroom and reliquary called the Treasury, which is filled with sacred vestments and liturgical furnishings that reveal the city's devotion to its patron Saint, the Madonna of the Letter. The treasures—precious gemstones and

SOUL TATTOOS

fabulous jewelry dating back to the Middle Ages—were given as sacrifice by the Crusaders' wives to the Madonna, imploring her for the lives of their heroic spouses, betrothed, and family members.

The museum-like exhibit rivals anything in the Smithsonian. It is full of statues, paintings, and icons of Mary that are draped with diamonds, pearls, rubies, emeralds, and semi-precious stones—all set in the most precious metals on Earth—offered up by the wealthiest and most regal women in the world at the time.

I had never given a thought to the women the Crusaders had left at home. They were the military wives of their day and formed a network of compatriots. United by a common bond (the love of their male partners, who were committed to the same cause), they were in a situation that was new, puzzling, lonely, and difficult. In Messina, they found what they needed: one another. That's what we all need.

THE GYPSIES
(THE ROMA)

(They originated in the Punjab region of India as a nomadic people and entered Europe around the eighth century. Called *Gypsies* because Europeans mistakenly believed they came from Egypt, this minority is made up of distinct groups called *tribes* or nations.)

"It is impossible to imagine a more complete fusion with nature than that of the Gypsy."

—Franz Liszt

(Hungarian composer, one of the greatest pianists of all time, best known for his "Hungarian Rhapsody No. 2.)

THE GYPSIES (ROMA)

Opportunists

As I returned to the Piazza, the square for gatherings, tourists were arriving for the twice-daily clock show. Messina's Cathedral has the largest and most complex mechanical and astronomical clock in the world. With its carousel of gilded bronze statues on the Bell Tower, the lion growls and the cock crows. As noon approaches, the square fills with tourists from around the world who are disembarking from motor coaches and from horse-drawn carriages, an expression of the Belle Epoque of Messina.

I didn't see how the Gypsies arrived. There was no caravan of horse-drawn wagons; there was only an energetic rush of men, women, and children, colorfully dressed who brushed against the tourists.

I must have been a gypsy in a former life. I love the music: the *jazz menarche,* the music of the Gypsy Kings, the soundtrack to a movie about a chocolatier, starring Johnny Depp, and Cher's song about thieve, tramps, and gypsies. I love flamboyant gypsy attire and the free-flowing scarves. I love their free-wheeling willingness to jump into an occasion and not hold back. I can pick pockets—playfully, not for profit—at a cocktail party and return wallets, without emptying them, to my unsuspecting guests.

Knowing some common gypsy scams, I warned my travel companions not to stoop down to pat the puppy, not to scream when a gypsy threatens to drop her baby, and to avoid being bumped, shuffled, and pilfered.

So, when a little girl ran up to me, I just knew it was her job to distract me so her brother could take something from my purse or backpack. I shouted at her, pointed my index finger at her, and used the voice I reserve for a life-and-death situation, "No!" She never came in my direction again.

I felt sorry for her. I knew she was trapped in her Romani culture, educated to be streetwise, a hard worker, a breadwinner, and a charming decoy who could sing, dance, entertain, and captivate an audience of one or a whole tour bus.

I have an obligation to that little girl, as I do for all the children of the world. We all do. They need to be educated and to maximize their inherent talents in order to become productive, positive members of society. She had, undoubtedly, a gift for languages, and could understand and recognize the countries of origin of her marks.

Children like to learn. Let us provide proper role models and teachers to set and keep all children on the right track.

Synchronicity is a term originally coined by psychologist Carl Jung that refers to the meaningful (or even miraculous) coincidences that occur in your life.

(Carl Jung was the Psychologist who founded analytical (Jungian) psychology and clustered people into introverts and extroverts.)

THE BLACKSMITH

Synchronicity

After watching the clock performance, I began my hunt for the best seafood meal of my life. I had been anticipating the sights of Sicily's renowned preparations and the taste of fish—raw or cooked, sardines or swordfish—and I was ready for my tastebuds to be tantalized. I walked away from the cathedral, heading to the left. One block later, I stopped in my tracks, not for a restaurant, but for something I found so intriguing that it became, not a diversion, but my *raison d'être*.

The blacksmith's doors were flung wide open, exposing a workshop full of benches, tools, contraptions suspended from the ceiling, wooden barrels, and an open flame with an overhead hood. The smithy himself, wearing a welding helmet with a rectangular lens, stood at an anvil in front of his workshop. Having just come from the cathedral, my mind set on the Crusaders and their lives, here—in the flesh—stood the vision of my hero incarnate. His arms were swarthy, hairy, and sweaty. His blue work shirt was open at the collar, and he wore a leather apron.

He pounded a piece of metal rhythmically, then thrust the object into a barrel of water;

SOUL TATTOOS

it sizzled and sputtered. I watched, fascinated. When he stopped, he pivoted the faceplate onto the top of his head, saw me watching, and chuckled. He was friendly and started a conversation that I could not understand. With sweeping arm movements, I pantomimed my admiration for the workshop and his hard work.

He removed his helmet and leather gloves and guided me to enter the shop to the right. In that corner, finished products, which were displayed on a clean workbench, had descriptions (in Italian, of course) and cards with prices stated in Euros. A fascinating array of objects of hand-forged matte-black wrought iron, sharpened steel, and polished brass and silver seemed as if they had time-travelled to his bench. I lifted several for a closer look. He gave me explanations, that I somehow understood. He wiped pieces with a jewelers' rouge in order to buff them and remove fingerprint smudges as I returned them to their arrangement.

We continued our walk to the rear of the workshop, which smelled of oily metal, like an auto mechanic's workshop. He would occasionally demonstrate how an object was used, just as he did to show how bellows fan the flame. He allowed me to put on a welder's helmet. I was happier than if I had been allowed to model the most resplendent and famous coronation crown from the Crown Jewels in the Tower of London. He brought me to a mirror. That was the real me!

I returned to the finished objects and handed him my favorite piece: an intricate wheel with six brass bells, to be attached to a wall. It was operated by cranking the handle to ring the bells. It sounded like sounds, which I remembered from my childhood, at Mass when the altar boy would ring the bells as the priest presented the holy sacrament. The bells are my daily reminder as I ring them when I enter my kitchen. The blacksmith made my visit to Messina perfect. I had been catapulted into one of the best medieval movies: Ridley Scott's.

The blacksmith could easily have been Balion (Orlando Bloom's role), the twelfth century French village blacksmith during The Crusades. (Learning his birthrate as he was the son of Crusader Lord Godfrey of Ibelin, Balion accepted the crusader's life offered to him solely in order to receive divine forgiveness, as promised to all crusaders who defended Jerusalem from invaders. Instructed in the skills of war and the chivalric honor code, he proved his worth as a superior fighter and noble idealist in the service of the king.)

I met the man who could have been a real-life version of a character in the movie that had impelled me to go to Messina. There are no coincidences. Synchronicity is *The Science Behind Coincidence*. Everything in our life is linked—from the past to the present and future—and every single coincidence or accident we stumble upon is linked. No matter how small or big a movement is, it is all about synchronicity.

"When the student is ready, the master appears" is a concept applied to individuals earlier in this book. That is how synchronicity is explained. Whenever we are synchronized with something we truly want, we are more likely to meet with it This is why similar people meet accidentally; they are tuned in to the exact same frequency, and synchronicity does its best to match them.

Synchronicity is like a mirror—whatever we believe in will reflect back to us. Agreeing with the law of syncing is all that is needed to connect and send messages on a spiritual level. Understanding synchronicity translates to establishing harmony in everything that we seek. Coincidence is only an illusion. Past, present, and future are all linked. We may not understand everything that happens to us, but there is always a reason, and that reason becomes apparent at some point in time.

Carl Jung taught that Synchronicity is a reality that is ever present for those who have the eyes to see. Synchronicity is spiritual and universal intelligence that is trying to teach us, reach us, and share love, support, and guidance. Learning to be open to synchronicity brings great surprises, like meeting a blacksmith in Messina.

THE SWEET SICILIAN LADY

"All you need is love. But a little chocolate now and then doesn't hurt."

—Charles M. Schulz

(American cartoonist and creator of the comic strip "Peanuts," featuring the characters Charlie Brown and Snoopy, among others.)

THE SWEETS LADY IN SICILY

Nurturance

I departed the blacksmith's shop and proceeded downhill, heading away from the historic Duomo region and towards the slip where my cruise ship was docked. I continued my quest for the perfect Sicilian seafood lunch. One promising restaurant after the next had menus in Italian—a good sign of authentic Italian cooking for Italians, as it's not aimed at tourists. Everything was closed! It was a Monday, but it was *Easter* Monday, a bank holiday in Europe. I was devastated. My stomach was growling; I had to find something. I came upon a convenience-kind of store with outdoor cafe tables and chairs. According to the pictures, the shop featured ice cream. Inside, there was a refrigerated, lighted pastry showcase with several shelves. I pantomimed to the lady behind the counter. Yes, she had made all of them.

I don't have a sweet tooth, but Sicily is renowned for its pastries, especially starting with the cannoli. Different from our American version (and tastier), the sheep's milk ricotta gives theirs the characteristic tanginess.

SOUL TATTOOS

I couldn't decide! Each piece enticed me with its shape, the filling, or the embellishment. The aroma overall smelled heavenly. Sicilian sweets specialities are known as The Scent of Sicily. I knew the names of some of their ten most famous, but there were so many different styles that I had never seen before, which made for a confectionary quandary. I couldn't lose. Whatever I selected would be extraordinary. Finally, I pointed to my choice, and she shooed me out so she could serve me at a table on the sidewalk. It took her such a long time to pour me a cup of coffee and serve a pastry, but I was happy to wait since I had, after all, found something so delectable before returning to the ship.

Finally, I heard shuffling of feet, rattling of plates and silverware, and humming. The lady appeared with a huge tray that a waiter would normally use to serve a whole tableful of hungry diners. Laden with one piece of everything in the pastry showcase, the tray presented a Sicilian pastry sampler for me! She beamed and arranged each plate onto my table and the table next to mine.

She talked non-stop, describing, gesturing, taking a portion on a fork or spoon, and feeding me one mouthful, one example, one bite at a time! I'm sure I must have been fed as an infant, but certainly not as an adult. She was nurturing—an Earth Mother—awaiting a reaction after delivering every taste sensation. I gave verbal and non-verbal responses to the most angelic tastes. Sounds, hand gestures, and eye-rolling in delight came naturally. So did the next bite of the next delectable treat. I couldn't choose a favorite, unless I chose her. For she was the sweetest in all of Sicily, I am sure.

My day in Messina had elements of the expected and unexpected, the planned and the spontaneous. The day was filled with people shining their lights and presenting their best sides to a stranger by being themselves, no prompting required. It was a day of authenticity and joy, a day of sweetness.

MONTSERRAT, SPAIN

(A Benedictine monk retreat within the one hundred
peaks of the Pyrenees. Associated in the Middle Ages
with Parsifal's search for the Holy Grail.)

***A magical sense
surrounds your body
and mind in an aura
of mystical tranquility.***

(The natural park is formed by needles
and monoliths of calcareous formation
that act like powerful antennas that emit
frequencies of geobiological magnetism.)

THE BLACK MADONNA

Beauty in Nature

A sunny day in Barcelona proved to be perfect for this pilgrim's journey to see a thirty-eight-inch twelfth-century wooden statue with jet-black faces and miraculous healing powers, purportedly carved by St. Luke. Residing an hour away in the Benedictine mountain retreat of Montserrat, Spain, The Black Madonna, a carved medieval image of the Virgin holding the Christ Child, is a Mystery of the Ages, representing the darkness contained within the Queen of Nature and in ourselves.

Examples of the Black Madonna are found all over the world. Some estimate that there are around five hundred Black Madonnas in Europe alone, mostly portrayed as Byzantine icons and statues in Catholic and Orthodox countries.

The shrines and images of the Black Virgin have an undeniable spiritual power, which explains their attraction for tourists, as well as those seeking a cure for their ills.

Having researched and written about the Black Madonnas for years, I was overjoyed with the prospect of seeing one for myself. After a bus ride through the picturesque countryside of

Catalonia (with spectacular mountain views and unusual rock formations), I took the funicular to the Holy Grotto, which is at an elevation of 4,000 feet.

The courtyard of the basilica held hundreds of swarming pilgrims. I learned that it was a church holiday with special mass being said, so crowds were larger than usual. I was a little panicky when the entrances to the basilica were blocked by throngs of worshippers. I became a rude American tourist, wheedling my way through a sardine-close mass of worshippers who were standing in spaces between pews. I reached the stairway entrance to see the Madonna. The sign on the chain read *Closed during service*. I traced the line of pilgrims from that door through the entire building, and to the exit. Cutting in line was not possible. I walked to the end but knew that time prevented my seeing the Madonna and catching my bus ride back to Barcelona.

I was devastated. I stood in the courtyard and bawled unconsolably. Everyone in line, not yet inside the basilica, was watching me. The priest at the head of a group smiled at me and started singing a hymn. His flock joined him in song. He walked to me and wiped away my tears with his thumb as if he were anointing me. He blessed me. Still singing, his parishioners came to me one at a time and hugged me, or kissed my hand, or patted my shoulders.

I felt a kinship and realized that they would visit the Madonna on my behalf! I was consoled.

SOUL TATTOOS

They were still singing and waving to me from their line, which had still not yet begun to move. I walked away, heading to catch my bus. It was sunny, but a ferocious wind howled. I looked up to the mountain top. The rock formations looked like cartoon mounds of soft-serve ice cream with faces. Animated, open eyes and mouths mimicked blowing tempestuous wind. The mountain mounds formed the shape of the Black Madonna!

I did not see the carved Madonna indoors, but the natural Earth Mother presented herself to me in all her resplendent, unpredictable, unforeseeable splendor, gazing benignly on me and all of the other pilgrims. The Black Madonna spoke from the mountain at Montserrat that day, speaking through the wind, the special mass, the pilgrims' devotion, and the priest's song.

Sometimes things are not the way we expected, or planned, or envisioned. Sometimes they are better.

AMSTERDAM

"What's special about Amsterdam is that the city is able to connect worlds that are not otherwise connected."
—Marcel Wanders

(Dutch architectural, interior and industrial designer.)

AMSTERDAM

Rejuvenation

"You're dying," the cardiologist told me as I lay in the hospital bed. The effects of rheumatic fever, which I had had as a child, had caught up with me.

The doctors told me that I couldn't do anything athletic. It's a good thing I didn't know that. I had climbed all of the 4,000-foot peaks on the Appalachian Trail in New England during both summer and winter, rappelled down cliffs, skied in the Alps, and engaged in countless other activities I hadn't known were bad for my heart.

He shouted at me, "You're gonna *beg* me for surgery!" As he stormed out of the room, I called a friend, packed up my things, and left the hospital.

I told Robbi I had never been on a cruise, but that I was dying, so I might as well kick the bucket while having a last adventure. I asked her if she would like to take a cruise, and she said sure! I looked on a website that had arranged several of my European low-priced, last-minute escapades. I found a North Atlantic cruise leaving in three days.

SOUL TATTOOS

We packed, not knowing what to expect on a cruise ship that would take us to countries that we had never seen: Norway, Sweden, Denmark, Finland, Latvia, Estonia, and Russia. We were departing from the Netherlands. I was excited.

We flew to Amsterdam, and I was reminded of the last flight I had taken.

I had been bumped to first class by customer service. The first thing the flight attendant did after I buckled in was to hand me a glass of champagne. In first class, you have to pace yourself. Champagne was followed by food and more to drink. I looked down. Blood was running from my knee to my ankle. What a way to go! I had no regrets. I wasn't in any pain; I was doing what I loved best: traveling. I didn't ask if there was a doctor on board. I wiped my leg and realized it wasn't blood; it was red wine. To my relief, the attendant's, and everyone else's in first class, I said I was cutting myself off; no more drinks for me. I arrived safely and in good condition to proceed with my life.

On this trip, Robbi and I flew coach to Amsterdam to board the ship. We had arrived a day early to be sure we didn't miss the boat. My legs swelled on the long flight. It was painful to walk, but we had to see the sites. We visited the Van Gogh Museum, the infamous red-light district, and Amstel, the street that runs along the river and has iconic colorful buildings.

When I couldn't walk any further, we asked at the canal if we could board a boat to take us to our hotel. The owners were closing up for the day. We talked to the two towheaded owners; they had pageboy haircuts and resembled a grown-up version of the Dutch Boy Paint logo.

After a long, friendly conversation, they told us they were on their way home now, and they could drop us at a trolley stop. We accepted gratefully. We were enjoying every minute, having a memorable cruise along the canal, as they provided commentary and indicated the mayor's house and other notable sites, including the Anne Frank house. They pointed out the bridge made famous by Van Gogh's painting. Our hosts described how they had renovated the *Valentinjn* and named their boat after the day they had purchased it. We had such a good time together!

The skipper's name was Arno. I asked him if that was the same as the river in Italy. He said yes, as that was where he was born. When we reached the end of the canal, they showed us where to catch the trolley. We hugged our hosts and said thank you and goodnight. (They would not accept any money. They said they were going that way anyway.)

The next day, Robbi and I reversed course and took the trolley back to where we had boarded the previous night. We bought tickets and stood in line waiting to enter The Anne Frank House. Only a few are admitted at a time.

We stood in line with people from several different countries and overheard many different languages.

SOUL TATTOOS

There was not much canal traffic. Then I spotted the *Valentinjn*, with Arno at the steering wheel, his elbow out the open window, transporting a boatload of disinterested passengers. They were keeping to themselves, not talking. Normally, I am quiet and reserve shouting for life-or-death situations, which I have had to use on occasion, but I shouted in full voice, "Arno!" He looked like a meerkat as he poked his head out the window and perked up his head, looking left and then right. He spotted me in the crowd. As his partner joined him, we all waved. Arno blew me a kiss. I caught it. I blew him a kiss, and he caught it and held it to his heart. That's what travel is all about: recognizing that wherever in the world we are from, we are all connected.

I've saved a birthday card that Robbi gave me, with cutouts of characters on The Yellow Brick Road. It says, "It's not where you go, it's who you meet along the way. I'm happy our paths crossed and even happier we're friends." It is a tribute to our friendship and the fact that we have visited many countries together.

In The Anne Frank House, the staircase is narrow and steep. It took every ounce of my strength, with my huffing and puffing, to reach the room where Anne Frank had to hide. The energy in the room was charged. People automatically entered in silence. There was so much sadness and empathy from the many visitors over the years. Her room has teenage-girl trappings of the era, including the original faded floral wallpaper that has magazine covers of the stars at the time—notably, one with Queen Elizabeth as a teen. I spent a long time staring out the window at the tree Anne Frank must have watched every day. I was fascinated by it, too.

It had been an emotional two days of linking past and present, and old and new friends.

INDIA

"The Indian way of life provides the vision of the natural, real way of life. We veil ourselves with unnatural masks. On the face of India are the tender expressions which carry the mark of the Creator's hand."

—George Bernard Shaw

(Irish playwright, wrote Pygmalion, which was adapted into the Broadway musical *My Fair Lady*.)

THE ORPHAN

"The weak fall, but the strong will remain and never go under."

—Anne Frank

(From *The Diary of a Young Girl*.)

THE ORPHAN

An Artist with Many Gifts and Talents

On one spiritual journey to India, I visited the historic, holy city of Vrindavin, the birthplace of Lord Krishna—the Hindu god of compassion, tenderness, and love—and one of the most popular and widely revered among Indian divinities. Vrindavin, the City of Widows, is a scourge of India filled with six-*thousand* widows dressed in white, the color of mourning, thronging the dirt streets, begging. Cast out by their families, these pilgrims, usually elderly women, are from throughout India; some have traveled hundreds of miles. They wander in and out of the many temples, aimlessly living out the rest of their lives.

Widows in India no longer throw themselves on their husbands' funeral pyres, but life for the widows, nonetheless, ends upon the death of their spouses. Deemed inauspicious, many of these women soon find they have lost their income and are ostracized in their home villages. Some are sent away by the husbands' families, who want to prevent them from inheriting money or property. Some come as pilgrims to devote their remaining years to the service of Krishna, but many others come to escape being flung out by their families like unwanted baggage.

In Vrindavin—amidst the hordes of women in a bleak environment—lies the gated and guarded 52-acre community called VatsalyaGram, an orphanage and progressive template not only for India but also for society. It is a happy village of unconditional love set in daycare and residential facilities of "forever families" in a world of love, education, and healthcare for those in need.

A guard holding a long gun blocks the entrance. Our driver presents a letter to the guard, who reads it and raises the barrier with a wave and a flourish, bowing. In VatsalyaGram, the mood changes instantly to a feeling of growth and hope. We drove on paved streets past crops, a complex of buildings, construction sites, and smiling faces of children who were walking leisurely. This was the embodiment of Reverend DiDi Maa Sadhvi Ritambhara's vision: to bring change to society through dedication and commitment. Her imagination was transformed into an actual place where underprivileged, abandoned children now live a normal and happy life.

She created a facility of "homes" for thirty children of different ages, each with a college-educated "mother" and a "grandmother"—role models and mentors—forming emotional bonds within a family and providing an education giving wings to young lives, empowering them to explore heights of social and economic challenges.

Some babies arrive and are accepted at VatsalyaGram as soon as three hours after being born. There is a little revolving door. A bell is rung sounding when a child has been left. A child up to thirteen-years-old will be accepted into the fold immediately. The children are given resources for growth and development in a safe environment, securing India's future as they are inducted into mainstream society.

Sadhvi Ritambhara envisions a country where all children can be happy. VatsalyaGram in Vrindavin is the prototype. It is being replicated in several locations in India, allowing more children hope for the future. It is a top NGO in India, offering education and healthcare.

Women are given vocational training to be self-reliant and self-confident by learning trades —such as making and canning jam, and making and packaging rosewater (from roses they cultivate), designing and sewing clothing, and caring for small and large animals. VatsalyaGram has a herd of 175 cows, which are sacred in India. The milk is used for nourishment for the children.

The women were as fascinated with us as we were with them. They huddled together, walking as if they were connected, holding on to a rope, as children in kindergarten would, being led to cross the street. The women were delighted to show us what they were doing. They were surprised that we were taking an interest in them. They were washing jars for honey (they had collected from their hives) and for jam (which they make from strawberries grown on the property). They showed us garments they had sewn, to be sold or would be worn by families in VatsalyaGram. One woman had designed a dress. She beams with pride while showing us. There was no language barrier. No spoken language was needed.

We stayed several days in this model village and were being treated like foreign dignitaries. Sally Perry, our group's spiritual leader, had been connected with VatsalyaGram for many years. She knew DiDi Maa and also Swami Parmanand, who oversees the foundation. The children are all given Swami Parmanand's last name.

The students, aged six to sixteen, welcomed us, entertained us, and demonstrated their academic and music skills with performances they had prepared for us. We were seated in the courtyard and were treated to dramatic readings (in English) and to instrumental and voice presentations of bhajan (hymns in Hindi).

We were brought to classrooms for "Show and Tell." It was equally enlightening for us to see *sixty* perfectly attentive, sardine-packed classmates sitting cross-legged on the floor for class as it was for them to see us and hear what we sounded like. They smiled for the camera, for us, and just because they were happy kids.

We also visited the homes—each with a mixture of thirty boys, girls, and parental figures—all acting like families at home anywhere. They talked, teased each other, and beamed with pride for each other's accomplishments. The atmosphere was trusting and safe.

Neeraj Mehta—our guide and Sally Perry's friend of many years, who works at VatsalyaGram— brought us to classrooms for the oldest children, where the students were conducting science projects in one room and practicing traditional music on musical instruments in another room.

He told some girls in one class that I am an artist. The following day, one girl had a gift for me: a painting of the blue Lord Krishna with his flute. It had been simply and painstakingly crafted. I knew she had painted it and that it was her prized possession. She touched my heart. In a place where people had nothing, she was giving me a lesson. The temptation was for me to refuse the gift since it was precious to her. But I had learned my lesson from another girl the same age in another country. I had failed that lesson by not being gracious enough to accept her gift of a painting.

I had to accept this painting of Lord Krishna and let this girl know I valued the painting and I was grateful to her for presenting it to me. There was an important lesson that we were all witnessing in this moment. This girl was wealthy beyond compare. She owns the Kingdom of Heaven, and she was opening the curtain so we could see into that world.

The Kingdom of God is so valuable that losing everything on Earth, but getting the Kingdom, is a happy trade-off. All is love. That is all that matters. She knew it, and she was teaching us the lesson with Godlike precision.

SOUL TATTOOS

I think of her often and hope she is happy in her world, somewhere in India now. She is an example of the success of DiDi Maa's vision to re-establish Indian civilization by giving people a better life and a brighter tomorrow. This young girl has a bright and shining future. She has learned the lesson that VatsalyaGram instills: that dealing with social and economic challenges begins by empowering people. The Artist was empowered, and she demonstrated her ability to empower me and all who witnessed her act of generosity and grace.

CLOSE TO HOME

*"I'm ready to
accept the challenge.
I'm coming home."*

—Lebron James

("King James" is an American professional basketball player for the Los Angeles Lakers.)

PETER BRANCH

"A friend in need is a friend indeed."

—Quintus Ennius

(Roman poet who lived in second century B.C.E.)

PETER BRANCH

A Friend Indeed

What else could I do when facing an imminent housing crisis? Right! Throw a party!

When I was a graduate student at The College of William and Mary, I found myself in a new environment and a new financial situation. I received a graduate assistant stipend and was fortunate enough that friends offered me a place to live for $50 a month. There's always a catch! I had to relinquish the cottage on the Chickahominy River in Toano, Virginia, during the summer months. I needed somewhere to live during my landlords' summer vacation on the river.

So I had a party with a purpose: to find somewhere to live between Memorial Day and Labor Day. I invited friends from two camps: "Town and Gown," which is how academics refer to a university, and its non-academic neighbors.

I invited professors and students from William and Mary. I also invited my new friends from the river, whom I called "The Chickahominy Chainsaw Boys." They were rough and tough, until they let me get to know them. Then they revealed sides often hidden from others: warmth, compassion, and generosity beyond belief. These were men who would give a friend-in-need the shirts off their backs, their last dollar, or the last piece of beef jerky!

This party was a meeting of extroverts and introverts, outdoor folks, and academics sheltered by the "stacks" (of books in Swem Library).

One of my neighbors was Peter Branch, a ninety-year-old former tugboat captain from North Africa.

I had met Peter Branch one day that previous Fall. He was walking my neighbors' dog. I hadn't seen him before, so I introduced myself and asked if I could help him. He told me his name and said the Holts would be home late, and they had asked him to walk their pampered poodle, Taffy.

Peter seemed like a character. He had twinkly eyes and an easy smile. On a whim, I invited him to my Christmas get-together, which I was having later that evening. He accepted. I told him I needed greens for the party. He said, "Hop in my truck, and I'll get you some." Perfect.

We drove around the power lines and down roads I hadn't noticed or explored yet. We ended up at Peter's house. He opened his garden gate and was chopping some big leafy crop. I asked, "Peter, are you cutting those for your supper?"

He looked at me, confused. "You said you wanted greens! These are for you."

"I meant greens to decorate for the party! I need a tree and roping and pine branches and things with red berries." In Boston, those are greens! In the South, greens are those earthy leaves boiled with fatback in *potlikker*.

So we drove around some more, and he brought me to his secret ring of faerie moss. He collected some for me. I was delighted. We stopped for other natural ornaments that we could add to the overflowing basket in the back of the truck.

That party was festively decorated and a success. It was the first gathering of disparate individuals whose paths might never have crossed otherwise.

The party in May to find me housing was a renewal of those new friendships, a continuation of unfinished conversations, and a delightful gathering. But there was business at hand. I asked, in front of friends and neighbors, "Who knows where I can live during the Summer?" No one had anything to say.

"Well, why don't you live with me?" asked Peter gruffly. There was silence. I didn't have a good reason not to accept his bold request. I accepted! There was a unanimous cheer, pats on the back, witty remarks, and a quick return to conversations, food, fun, and festivities.

I settled in at Peter's cozy cottage, which was on a creek that fed into the river. The scenery was simple; nature provided bird sightings and sounds; a beaver would occasionally surface among the marsh reeds. Peter was a great host that summer. He would serve me coffee and breakfast, and he hosed down my windshield before I left for campus every morning. When I returned at the end of my work/study day, he would have a cold rum and coke waiting for me. I asked his secret for making that drink so tasty. An extra tablespoon of sugar! Yikes!

Peter Branch was just like his rum and coke: He was a sweet surprise!

JIMMY SPARRER

"To be blind is not miserable; not to be able to bear blindness, that is miserable."

—John Milton

(He was blind, one of the greatest English poets, and is best known for *Paradise Lost*, the greatest epic poem in English.)

JIMMY SPARRER

Skipper Extraordinaire

"Jump in!" Without hesitation, I stood on the edge of the boat and jumped into the water, just as the blind man had ordered me. I couldn't swim, but I trusted him.

He had first stretched out along the edge of the boat and reached into the water, swishing his *deafblind*—his red-and-white-striped cane. I did not need further explanation. I had already spent half an hour in the boat, which he skippered quickly around pilings and homemade navigational markers in the channel, using memory as well as any seeing-eyed skipper would have used his vision. Jimmy was blind, but he could see from his lifetime memory.

Later, I would learn that Jimmy had served in the U.S. Navy during World War II, specifically in the Pacific theater aboard the U.S.S. Topeka. He was a student at the NASA Langley apprentice school when a hunting accident left him permanently blinded. He subsequently transferred to the photographic department at NASA Langley, where he developed pictures of the moon landings and many other historic events, which he enjoyed talking about in detail but which he had, ironically, never seen.

A boatload of fishermen and I boarded Jimmy's boat, moored at the pier at his house. I had fished gill nets on the Chickahominy River with Ernest, and Ollie, and some of the other men when the herring were running. Several women, some of them wives, prepared food inside, but I was invited to fish in the jon boat.

They were all practical jokers, and that day's clammers wanted to scare me, but I trusted Jimmy from the first day I met him. Everyone was surprised I jumped. They followed suit matter-of-factly. This was not their first rodeo. Jimmy stayed with the boat and anchored it.

Someone had already pitched the gear for all of us into the water. I was handed one complete set, consisting of a clam rake and an inner-tube with a net attached to it, tethered to a rope that I tied around my waist.

Everyone wanted to demonstrate to me how to catch a clam. There were five instructors per one student: me. They gave me directions to follow: Walk in the waist-deep water of the Chesapeake Bay; Never lose sight of the boat, as it's our ride home, and Drag your feet along the sandy bottom, feeling for a clam. Got one! The next instructions: Rake it up, and, Toss it up into the air, aiming for the net in the tire! Score! The net would fill with the clams. The final instruction: Walk around, dragging the net through the water on the way to capturing the next clam. The catch would cleanse itself of sand before being loaded back onto the boat.

I was off on my own, enjoying playing that game, the sunshine, the cool water, and the scenery. The men all set off for deeper waters. When we had reassembled and climbed the little ladder onto the boat, I was disappointed that the clams I caught were so small! The men's were all much larger. I didn't know why they were laughing, but they started shucking my catch so we could enjoy it before we were skippered back. The young, smaller clams were tender, sweet morsels; and they tasted the best. They tasted like dainty bites given up by King Neptune himself.

Jimmy Sparrer was a marvel. A keen sportsman, he was an avid fisherman, catching his last cobia at the age of eighty-four. Fishing was not his only skill. An experienced woodworker, he made and gave away hundreds of bluebird nesting boxes. Bluebirds are symbols of joy and happiness, a reminder of all the beauty of nature. It is only natural that the sight of a bluebird reminds me of Jimmy and that joyous day of raking clams on the Chesapeake Bay.

ARNOLD HUDGINS

"Carpe diem."
(in Latin, translated to "Seize the day.")

—Horace

(Taken from Book 1 of the Roman poet's *Odes*, 23 BC.)

ARNOLD HUDGINS

Retired Merchant Mariner

"This is yours, honey." He didn't say much. We didn't talk a lot. Arnold and I would sit on his front steps and wave to the drivers who passed by the house and honked their horns to say hello. Anyone who drove down Bethel-Peniel Road was "a local." Mathews County didn't have strangers. There were "come-here" folk, but they couldn't help it. They didn't have the foresight to be born in this throwback to the 1950s.

I first saw Arnold Hudgins on his wedding day. I was dressed to attend his wedding. He was dressed in a Southern gentleman's uniform of grey flannel slacks, a navy blazer, a white shirt, and a classic striped tie. He was tall and lanky, like Ichabod Crane. He walked slowly, hunched over, showing his age of eighty-nine years.

I caught a brief glimpse of him; he was not looking at anyone, but he was just plodding along the path to the church.

The bride was nowhere to be seen. This was her burial day.

SOUL TATTOOS

Arnold and his intended had been lovers for years. They kept their romance secret, but everyone knew. Maybe even her husband, the lighthouse keeper, knew. I know only that after he passed away, the lovers set a wedding date for soon after. This was that day.

I didn't actually meet Arnold until the following week. I was extending my sympathies to the sister of Arnold's bride-to-be. She asked me to visit Arnold and cheer him up. I consented and drove to his farmhouse. It was love at first sight. We didn't say much. He did suggest, "Let's sit on the steps." We sat on the front steps for hours that day and whenever I was in Mathews. We would sit silently and point at the dragonflies, the wild turkeys, the hummingbirds, any pretty birds, or anything interesting that entered our field of vision. We didn't say anything; but we just nodded in appreciation, of sharing a visual gift presented to us courtesy of Mother Nature.

Arnold couldn't answer all of my questions. He didn't know why some fiddler crabs in the ditch by the road were right-handed and some were left-handed. He remembered the stable had held his horses, but he couldn't recall their names. He did know the grapes on the vines were scuppernongs. He used to plant crops, but then, for years, he mowed the seven-acre fields so they would look presentable on his land, which was sandwiched between two churches.

Arnold lived a simple, rural life. It ended simply and quickly. He was a broken man, having lost his true love and after coming so close to living out their dream. One evening, the police scanner blared out the call for an ambulance. I heard the address needing the rescue squad. I rushed to Walter Reed Medical Center, where I was allowed to stand by Arnold's gurney as he was wheeled, unconscious, into the emergency room. The monitor beeped and flashed glaring numbers and jagged lines. I knew I was in the way, I knew that the prognosis was not good without being told, and I knew I had to hold his craggy hand until I was ordered to go to the Waiting Room. It was the eve of Easter. I stood there, numb. I did not feel anything. Then an arctic, bone-chilling breeze blew through my body. I had never felt anything like it. It was not a weather shift. It was not scary. It made me smile warmly.

When the nurse entered the Waiting Room, looking down sadly, she announced time of death as 12:20. I said, "No. It was 12:06." I had looked at the clock when I felt Arnold pass through me and pass on.

Arnold was true to his word. The fourteen-acre farm was mine. Staying at the house during renovations one night, the disconnected farmhouse phone on the kitchen wall rang. I know who was calling.

A MEDICAL UPDATE

"To me, every hour of the day and night is an unspeakably perfect miracle."

—Walt Whitman

(Poet and volunteer nurse for Civil War veterans.)

A MEDICAL UPDATE

A Miracle

I began *Soul Tattoos* with a Flashback of jumping off a cliff. Now I'll tell you about the wheelchair. When I was a child, we didn't go to doctors. I remember having been bedridden for a while, but I didn't know the reason. It was diagnosed later, when I was an adult, as rheumatic fever.

Over the years, as a result, I had heart complications, but they weren't enough to stop me from having adventures on mountains and on the high seas. I would huff and puff, and be the slowest person hiking uphill; but I atoned by racing downhill like a jack rabbit, as it was easier on my heart. Even on a flat surface, I could never walk and talk at the same time. Taking a walk with someone, I would walk a few steps, talk, and then walk some more—and then talk and.... That was normal for me.

In time, I had a few cardiac episodes that landed me in the hospital, with my heart racing more than two hundred beats a minute. I was monitored and not allowed to move. It was following one of those hospital stays that I went on what was to be my final adventure: a cruise with Robbi.

I recovered from each episode and continued my life. But about four years ago, I had trouble breathing. The nurse practitioner prescribed over-the-counter Flonase. I bought it and used it; but it didn't help. I sat upright in bed because I couldn't breathe lying down. I knew I would be going to the hospital. I inched my way to the shower, gasping and holding on to anything. I didn't have the strength to lift my leg over the side of the tub, so I hosed down in the room, knowing I was making a mess, but what else could I do? I called Susan, my neighbor, and she drove me to the emergency room. I was admitted immediately.

They acted fast, wrapped me in copper blankets, and called for a helicopter to airlift me to Sentara Heart Hospital in Norfolk. Fog prevented the helicopter from taking off, so the ambulance driver, with the siren blaring, broke land-speed records, driving through the Hampton Roads Bridge Tunnel in twenty-three minutes. I marveled that they were taking such extreme care of an ordinary person.

A team of the best surgeons and cardiologists saw me, read my charts and films from all of the previous tests, and called for another team to see me. I agreed to sign DNR (Do Not Resuscitate) papers so they would leave me alone and let me sleep.

The doctors said there was nothing that could be done for me, so they just arranged for me to spend my remaining few days in comfort.

In my final transport, I was brought to Newport News (at a normal driving speed and with no siren) and was taken to a facility (nursing home/hospice) where they met with me and gave me a "welcome home" package, not welcoming me to the facility, but to the afterlife! While I was there, I was bedridden; some of my closest friends (Robbi, Crys, and Ali) came to visit and say goodbye. My gifted friends (Ginger, Kathleen, Denise, and Kathie) performed energy work on me. Chapel members (Bill, Peggy, Carl, Izzy, and others) brought me a ceramic angel that says "Believe!" I did. I believed it was not the end.

I stayed thirty days—praying, meditating, and watching the television reality show where hopeful entrepreneurs pitch their ideas, hoping for financial backing.

And then my insurance ran out. Everyone was amazed I had lasted that long. I was released but had nowhere to go. I could not manage thirteen steps in my townhouse. I couldn't even take three steps. My friend Linda took me in to her home in Buckroe Beach. All on one level, I had a bedroom, bathroom, kitchen, sofa, and sunroom. Linda made every effort to care for me and feed me, but I couldn't eat a bite. She would set up an oatmeal station, where I only had to push the button on the microwave. From the moment Linda went to work (after settling me on the sofa) to the moment she came home, I had not moved from that spot.

Home Health Care came, checked my vital signs, and told me I had to go to the hospital immediately. I needed to see a cardiologist first. I was not going back to any of the five cardiologists who held no hope for me. My friend Crys reminded me of Dr. Albert A. Burton, MD, the husband of Kelley, a fellow board member at the Peninsula Fine Arts Center. I received an expedited appointment. My ex-husband came to Linda's, helped me into his car, and then pushed me in a wheelchair into Dr. Burton's office. He read my files, looked at my charts, and asked if I would like to try his idea. Yes! No one else had had an idea besides my demise. He checked me into the hospital and put me on a regimen of treatments and medicines. I lost forty pounds of fluid over Thanksgiving week. My new friends, Tonney and Teresa, came and smuggled me a tiny raisin pecan tart. I was able to eat again. It was the best Thanksgiving dinner ever.

Water around all of my organs had been shutting them down one by one. After that week of progress, Dr. Burton scheduled a meeting regarding innovative surgery to replace my mitral heart valve (original equipment) with a state-of-the-art titanium valve. The surgeon from India met with me and said there was a small chance of success. Surgery was scheduled. My ex-husband took care of me and drove me to the hospital days later. I have tiny veins. It took five nurses to insert the IV. They ordered needles for me from NICU (neonatal intensive care unit).

Surgery day came. When I awoke from the in-novative, minimally invasive surgery, I was talking and laughing with the surgeon. I knew I was well. He knew I was well. Crys was at my bedside. We talked about our hijinks on the French Riviera a few years earlier.

SOUL TATTOOS

My ex-husband played Florence Nightingale for the next 109 days. He was going to have a stair lift installed for me, but I was able to navigate twenty-two stairs easily after surgery.

Soon after, I returned home, and have lived a normal life ever since. I have exercised at the gym three times a week, walking three miles a day, doing yoga, using the rowing machine, and doing group exercise.

During Covid-19, now I'm at home like everyone else and am on my own exercise program.

I am healthy and well thanks to Dr. Burton, who is delighted with my progress and my strong heartbeat.

I can walk and talk at the same time. Something that people take for granted is a new thrill for me. I am grateful and give thanks for each day that I am allowed to live.

THE PEACE GRID

"The best way to find yourself is to lose yourself in the service of others."

—Mahatma Gandhi

(Mahatma means "Great Soul.")

(The "Father of India" was the leader of India's non-violent independence movement against British rule. In South Africa, he advocated for civil rights of Indians. Born in Porbandar, India, Gandhi studied law and organized boycotts against British institutions in peaceful forms of civil disobedience,)

THE PEACE GRID

In Conclusion

I've always felt that we are all connected. I call it the Peace Grid. You're on it. I'm on it. Everyone everywhere is on it. Whenever we do something, it has an impact on everyone.

Everyone we ever meet is important to us. We are important to everyone.

I want to close by giving you something important. Some of you already have this. Some of you don't need me to give it to you. Some of you will be reinforced by this:

I'm giving you permission to be who you are and to become who you want to be.

Sometimes you need someone to give you permission. Sometimes you need someone to tell you what to do and to tell you that you're entitled to be you. We can give ourselves and each other affirmations from within that we might never hear from someone else. The best gift you can give anyone is to be yourself and to grow into your own skin more every day. Encourage others to be themselves.

Let's find the courage and give each other support to be our authentic selves. All you can be is yourself. And isn't it time to stop being someone you're not? It's time to believe in yourself and know that **you** are a **Soul Tattoo**.

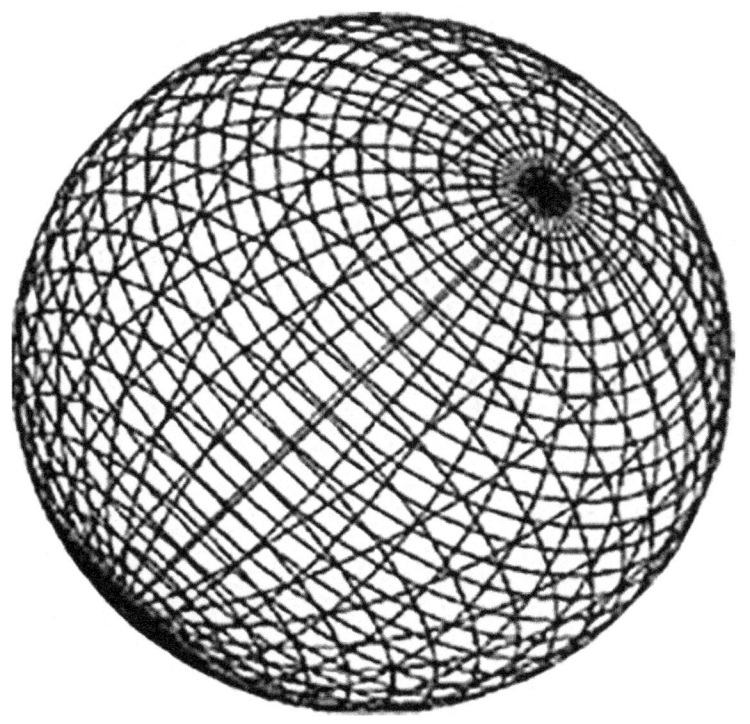

THE END
(for now...)

> *"Don't cry because it's over, smile because it happened."*
>
> —Dr. Seuss

(Theodor Seuss "Ted" Geisel was an American children's author, political cartoonist, illustrator, poet, animator, screenwriter, and filmmaker.)

THE END

(For now...)

So many more places, and so many more people have impacted my life than I have related to you in this book. There are adventures still to be experienced and new directions yet to take. I am forever open to possibilities. I have renewed my passport (with extra pages at no extra charge). I feel fortunate to have experienced planned and surprise encounters, and I will be delighted to tell you all about whatever transpires next. Until then,

I wish you love, courage, beauty, and more **Soul Tattoos!**

—Fran Walsh Ward

CREDITS (PHOTOS and GRAPHIC)

COVER CONCEPT, Carolyn Conway Riley

COVER PHOTO, Fran Walsh Ward

MOUNTAIN CLIMBING, Fran Walsh Ward

LOG CABIN, Pixabay from Pexels

THE WHITE HOUSE, Aaron Kittredge from Pexels

THE ARTIFACT, Fran Walsh Ward

COCONUT PALM, Fran Walsh Ward

KARAOKE, Fran Walsh Ward

GYPSIES, Miray Bostancı from Pexels

AMSTERDAM, Liene Ratniece from Pexels

LORD KRISHNA, Fran Walsh Ward

HEADSHOT, Fran Walsh Ward

THE PEACE GRID, Fran Walsh Ward

ABOUT THE AUTHOR
Fran Walsh Ward

"I like to make a snowman and throw snowballs at it."

My earliest recollection of speaking to a group was in first grade. The assignment was to stand in front of the room and tell something about ourselves. It was winter and bone-chilling cold in Cambridge. The first boy spoke and delivered that snowman address. Several others followed, each one repeated that first composition verbatim.

My turn came. "One day I went skating in the street."

(We left our faucets dripping overnight so the pipes wouldn't freeze. The firemen did the equivalent; the opened hydrants transformed Elm Street into an ice rink.)

Sister Patricia said I didn't say enough and asked me to tell more. I stood up from my seat again, walked to the front of the room, and said, "And I fell."

The class thought it was hilarious. Since then, I have been narrating my life's journey through my events—both commonplace and remarkable—whether they are of places—here, there, or anywhere—or involve personages. They are all unique.

Sister Patricia was the first person to encourage me to tell more. For a lifetime, as a teacher and a professor, as a writer and a speaker, I have used occurrences in my life as examples.

I am an author of an adventure/fantasy series (*Travels with Ellyn* and *Beyond the Drawbridge*) and nonfiction chronicle (*An American in Kashmir: Undaunted Love*), all written under my pen and given name Frances Ellen Walsh.

I have been a columnist of art and cultural reviews, previews, and interviews. I have given sermons based on my experiences, and I've been featured on radio broadcasts.

I live downtown in Hampton, Virginia, America's oldest continuous English-speaking town, dating to the early 1600s I tend to think I help perpetuate it's continuous speaking label.

I am more than an avid people-watcher. I interact. I am the observer and the observed. Einstein's Quantum Theory is simply about the very act of watching.

These **Soul Tattoos** are about my being the observer, being impacted by what I observe. We are all observers. We are all observed. Everyone we observe makes an impact on us. Since we all make a mark, we have a moral, ethical, and personal responsibility to be ourselves and to be the best we can be.

Travels with Ellyn
Paperback Edition
ISBN: 978-1-61244-262-4
Price: $15.95

Beyond the Drawbridge
Paperback Edition
ISBN: 978-1-61244-470-3
Price: $15.95

An American in Kashmir

Undaunted Love

Paperback Edition

ISBN: 978-1-61244-677-6

Price: $16.95

Made in the USA
Middletown, DE
22 December 2020